SUCCESSFUL DOG BREEDING

Also by Chris Walkowicz:

The Bearded Collie

SUCCESSFUL DOG BREEDING

Chris Walkowicz
and
Bonnie Wilcox, DVM

ARCO PUBLISHING, INC.
NEW YORK

Published by Arco Publishing, Inc.
215 Park Avenue South, New York, N.Y. 10003

Copyright © 1985 by Chris Walkowicz and Bonnie Wilcox, DVM

All rights reserved. No part of this book may be repro-
duced, by any means, without permission in writing from
the publisher, except by a reviewer who wishes to quote
brief excerpts in connection with a review in a magazine
or newspaper.

Library of Congress Cataloging in Publication Data

Walkowicz, Chris.
  Successful dog breeding.

  Includes index.
  1. Dogs—Breeding. I. Wilcox, Bonnie. II. Title.
SF427.2.W35 1985   636.7'0824   84-24247
ISBN 0-668-06134-0

Printed in the United States of America

10   9   8   7   6   5   4   3   2   1

This book is dedicated to our husbands,
Ed Walkowicz and Tom Wilcox,
who first interested us in mating and reproduction.

CONTENTS

- Muzzling
- Prolapsed Prepuce
- Artificial Insemination
- Multiple Sires
- Mismating/Mesalliance

- Palpating
- False Pregnancy
- Morning Sickness
- Touch Your Toes
- Feeding Expectant Mothers
- Resorption/Absorption
- Abortion
- Worms During Pregnancy
- The Labor Room

- Whelping Kit
- Nesting
- Listlessness/Restlessness
- Shivering
- Crying/Screaming
- Panting
- The Green Light
- Labor
- Simple Whelping
- Consuming Placentas
- Number of Pups
- The Birds and the Bees

- Vaginal Exam
- Prenatal Loss of Fetuses
- Primary Inertia
- Secondary Inertia
- Size of Litters
- Cesarean Section
- Malpresentation
- Getting a Grip on Things—Assisted Delivery
- Enormous Pups
- Prolapsed Vagina
- Prolapsed Uterus
- Uterine Torsion

FOREWORD

We hope that this book will save the serious breeder from being disheartened or from beating his breast when there are low points. He or she can learn from the past experiences of breeders who were kind enough to offer their advice and expertise in order to help others. We wish to thank the participants in our survey for cooperating with complete honesty. Because we promised them anonymity, we use "breeder" instead of their names.

Much of the material gathered in our survey appears throughout the text as examples, as well as in Appendix 1, which lists the occurence of breed tendencies and genetic predispositions.

Each dog is different, so a thousand stories can be told. We both thought that after twenty years' experience owning dogs, we were aware of every aspect of their breeding and whelping. We found there are more than a few left!

This book is meant not to replace your veterinarian but to supplement professional medical help. It is meant to be exactly what it is called: a handbook, that is, a book to be kept at hand. This handbook is a guide for the novice and a reference for the professional.

The breeder's best friend, next to your dog and your vet (and this handbook), are your records. Your record book will tell you many things the bitch can't. At the next whelping you will have an idea of what to expect. Don't trust your memory. After so many litters, things begin to run together. You'll wonder whether it was Flossie or Diva that whelped early.

Each whelping varies to some extent, although a bitch often sets a pattern from which she varies little. The same is true in breeding. Keep records of everything your bitch—or stud dog—does. Remember, the dogs don't read the book.

ACKNOWLEDGMENTS

Special thanks to our illustrator, Mary Jung, who so perfectly captured our every thought and brought it to life.

Great appreciation is also expressed to Carol Walsh Peterson for the two medical illustrations on pages 87 and 100.

SUCCESSFUL DOG BREEDING

1.   *TAKING THE FIRST STEP*

Should I or Shouldn't I?

The occasional breeder, also known as the novice or backyard breeder, does not have to be a poor breeder. On the contrary, the quantity of litters has nothing to do with the quality of the puppies produced.

A breeder can be professional in his or her breeding efforts even though he does not breed dogs often or as a business. In fact, commercial breeding practices carried to extreme, as in "puppy mills," are contrary to professionalism.

Whether breeding is your vocation or only an avocation, professionalism means that the breeder intends to produce healthy, attractive dogs. He refuses to mix breeds or to breed indiscriminately because of proximity, convenience, or financial appeal. There is no reason to perpetuate mediocrity.

A pro has researched the problems existing in his breed, and particularly in his own dogs. He is sure of the soundness of his breeding stock.

There is certainly a greater demand for pet puppies than for show puppies. However, a breeder does not have to strive to fill that demand, even if he is not interested in showing. The novice breeder should understand these facts: There will be a surplus of pet-quality puppies even in top show-quality litters, and while a show dog still makes a good pet, a pet-quality pup rarely makes a show dog.

Neutering

If you decide not to breed your dog, it is best to have it castrated or spayed. Neutering eliminates pesky seasons, unwanted pregnancies, straying, and lovelorn males. Desexing focuses the dog's attention on you, his owner, rather than on dogs of the opposite sex, and this in turn aids training the dog. It also avoids the stigma of the dog becoming an illegitimate parent.

The recommended minimum age for neutering is when the dog is between eight and eighteen months old, at puberty or sexual maturity. A clue to approaching puberty is the first season, or when leg-lifting commences. The hormones released at that stage cause the development of sexual characteristics, so that a male will still look like a male and a female will appear feminine after neutering.

Prepuberty neutering of the male can increase growth, since testosterone, the male hormone first released at adolescence, halts bone growth. Occasionally, the genitals of females spayed prior to puberty do not mature. As a consequence, eczema around the vulva can be a problem, because of urine irritation.

Neutering is a relatively simple and inexpensive operation and is certainly cheaper than an unwanted litter (or even than a much-desired litter). It is also easier than caring for puppies for a minimum of eight weeks.

It's been said that neutered dogs will become fat. Nothing makes them fat except too much food and lack of exercise. Watch food intake. As dogs mature, their bodies, just like ours, do not require as much food.

Some people advise not spaying a bitch until she has had a litter. That accomplishes nothing, especially since a dog does not have the human urge for maternity. Dogs never know when the joys of parenthood have passed them by.

Castration is the removal of the testicles from the scrotum. Spaying, or ovariohysterectomy, is the removal of the uterus and ovaries.

Although pregnancy may be avoided by a vasectomy or the removal of the uterus alone, those procedures do not eliminate the sexual urge or prevent the heat cycle.

Spaying stops recurrent false pregnancies and prevents uterine infections and cancer. It also decreases the likelihood of breast cancer.

Although neutering may help calm an overactive dog, maturity sometimes has the same effect. Castration helps curb the wanderlust and indoor urination. It prevents prostate problems and often checks aggression, particularly if done at puberty.

When you make an appointment for surgery, withhold food from the dog for twelve hours, otherwise it might become ill and vomit during anesthesia.

Recovery from neutering is swift, particularly if the dog is young and in good health. However, restrict its exercise and feed it mushy food for the first day. Your dog may feel so good that these will be your most difficult tasks.

Take your dog's temperature after any surgery. Normal rectal temperature is 101.5° F (38.6° C), or within a range of 100° to 102° F (37.8° to 38.9° C). A fever is often the first sign of infection or of other problems. Examine the incision for discharge, heat, or redness. Contact your vet if any of these symptoms appear.

The Pill and Other Options

Several factors could influence your decision to delay neutering. An altered animal cannot show in the breed ring, although it can compete in obedience. You might want to prevent a pregnancy temporarily. There are several alternatives available.

Disguising agents for heats, such as chlorophyll pills, Vicks Vaporub®, or commercial sprays, mask the odor and help control the attraction. These products do not curtail the breeding advances of the persistent female or male. They are an aid at shows or classes during the first and last days of season.

Oral birth control, the Pill for canines, is given only through veterinary prescription. This is an expensive method, though less so than unwanted puppies. The hormones in the Pill may cause the next season to be irregular. Owners' and pets' Pills are not interchangeable.

Tubal ligation, the tying of the fallopian tubes, prevents pregnancy but does not stop the heat cycle. A bitch still attracts males and can develop uterine problems.

Vasectomy, severing the vas deferens so the sperm cannot impregnate, is similar in effect to tubal ligation. The dog still has a sexual urge and response. There is no benefit other than that the testicles remain intact—and there are no paternity suits.

Of course, next to neutering, the best way to avoid pregnancies is to restrict the dating privileges of the female as well as the male. There is no safe time. Pregnancies have occurred on every day of the season. Males have been known to perform Olympian feats to obtain the lady of their dreams. Do not depend on a screen or fence to separate the lustful twosome. The only safe precaution is keeping both in security kennels or in crates, separated by solidly closed doors.

The Get-Rich-Quick Scheme

Breeding dogs is a costly business, if done right. It is even more costly—to your reputation—if done poorly.

Few make money in breeding, and none become rich. Most breeders are content to break even. Those who do make money usually sink their profits right back into the business.

A typical dream fades as follows: Your bitch whelps a normal healthy litter of five, and you see the dollar signs walking on their toddling legs. You sell the first pup, which pays for the lovely whelping box you built, the vet exam, and the first shots. The next sale goes for the food bill and advertising. The third pup covers the registration of the litter, pedigree forms, worming the pups, and the next shot.

You buy more food and more shots (seven for each pup in the first six months) while advertising for the last two prospective owners, wherever they may be. Finally, one more sells, which means you can reimburse your brother for the stud fee he loaned you. You cut the price to sell the last one (who by this point is out of his cute stage), and pocket the profit. That is, unless you have tail docking, dewclaw removal, ear cropping, or shipping expenses. Wait a minute. Did you forget to deduct the expense of purchasing the dam? You're in the hole.

Ah, but next time, you think. The bitch's price was covered by the last enlightening experience. You'll breed to a local stud and advertising won't be necessary because the last group of buyers will refer their friends and relatives.

So the pups come. Or rather *pup*, because it's a litter of one. That one goes as the pick pup to the stud owner, since you worked such a clever deal. But you must still pay the food bill, give shots, register, repaint the whelping box, etcetera, etcetera.

Well, this can't happen twice in a row, you think, so you breed the bitch on the next season. The vet said it'd be okay, since she only had one pup. You go back to the first stud, thinking it was likely the second stud's fault your bitch only had one pup. So you pay the fee, paint the box, buy food, and take reservations on the litter. The pups are born, everyone suddenly changes his mind, and the pups hang around for six months.

You buy a ton of food, give thirty-five shots, buy a large pen for the pups, and advertise, advertise, advertise. Then you must buy another pen to separate them because the girls are starting to come into season. Heaven forbid any of them get bred!

You finally manage to give the last two pups away, take a breather for a year and breed the dam again, figuring something good has to come of all this. After all, your bitch has three champions in her six-generation pedigree! She whelps eight pups. You have reservations for six of them at one hundred fifty dollars each. At last, you relax. However, they contract a virus for which there is no vaccine when they're six weeks old, before they can go to their new homes, and you lose all but three. Of course, you've already sunk a fortune into food, shots, and so on.

You have to keep the surviving three for another month since they might be contagious to other dogs, and it's cost you eighty-five dollars per pup for intravenous feeding to keep them alive. The six people cancel their reservations because (1) the pups aren't as cute at three months as they were at two, (2) they don't want a pup that's been sick, and (3) they already found one from their neighbor.

You're ready to give up and tell people you can't afford it any more.

You've never gotten a thing from all your work. Three years and nothing to show for it but bills.

Too bad.

If you'd counted the genuine affection from your pups, the loyal love from your bitch, some new friends you made along the way, the knowledge you've gained and could give to others, and the joy of watching puppies bounce after each other, maybe this story would have ended differently.

One did. A breeder reported the results of her first eight breedings:

1. No conception (commonly known as a miss).
2. Miss—spayed first bitch.
3. Lease of a bitch who died in labor from a ruptured diaphragm.
4. Miss (number 3 bitch).
5. Miss.
6. Number 4 bitch whelped, developed an infection, and killed the pups at two weeks, almost dying herself.
7. Back to number 3 bitch, who whelped. Milk went bad, pups were bottle-fed from five days. This bitch never conceived again.
8. Once again number 4 bitch, who whelped and raised a normal litter. Temperature elevated, but was controlled with antibiotics.

This devotee admits she felt a black cloud over her head, but persisted. Her record now shows eight years of breeding, with twenty litters to her credit.

Age

It doesn't matter how old *you* are. But it does make a difference how old the dog is. Sexual maturity is not a green light for breeding.

Although capable of breeding and conceiving at the first heat, the bitch is no more physically or mentally able to care for babies than the pubescent teenager. Neither is the "unbroken" stud wise in the mating procedure.

The American Kennel Club refuses to register progeny from sires under the age of seven months or over the age of twelve years. Likewise, the dams must be over eight months and under twelve years. Any litter conceived and whelped outside those age limitations must be attested to with reasonable proof and affidavit.

Most breeders recommend waiting until the second or third heat, around the age of eighteen months. If the bitch is to be a brood matron, she should be bred by three years of age. There is less flexibility of the pelvis and tissue with age, making it unwise to wait until the bitch is middle-aged to elderly before her maiden attempt at motherhood.

Top age for breeding depends on the health, condition, and breed. There are certain breeds—for instance, Miniature Schnauzers—that maintain fertility into advanced age. They often produce well with no ill effects at seven or eight years.

Studs can be broken in, depending on the breed and the inclination, between ten and fourteen months. Many studs continue to service bitches until the age of nine or ten (or older) with proper care and good health. Regular use of the stud is not recommended until two years.

Again, the Miniature Schnauzer holds off retirement. An owner wrote that her robust litter of five from a seven-year-old bitch and a ten-year-old stud is the latest in twenty-one get produced by the sire in four months. She states, "His vigor is astounding. He was a shy breeder when arriving here at five. No one could watch. Now I think he'd breed in a supermarket!"

Smaller breeds reach sexual maturity earlier than large breeds. Therefore, a Miniature Pinscher may be bred at a younger age than a Newfoundland.

The optimum age for breeding is the prime of life—two to five years. A commonly held but mistaken belief is that the best puppies are produced at the age of three. This may be because of being "in the prime" or because a stud is at the peak of his popularity. Good bitches are being sent to him, and he hasn't yet been challenged by the young bucks.

Litter size seems to increase until three or four years, when advancing age causes reduction in the size of litters. It is not uncommon for elderly bitches to go through a belated pregnancy only to produce a sole survivor.

A Firm Foundation—Soundness

A dog cannot function well in any arena—work, show, or pet—unless it is physically and mentally sound. Soundness is the ultimate prerequisite for a breeding animal. Any dog that is not totally sound should not be bred. There are no *buts*.

A dog with a severe physical defect, such as elbow or hip dysplasia, Von Willebrand's disease, esophageal or heart defects, or epilepsy, passes such hereditary ailments on to its progeny. X rays are the only positive method of diagnosing hip or elbow dysplasia. Unless deterioration is severe, afflicted dogs may live a fairly normal (though celibate) life.

Mental soundness is also hereditary, and only dogs with stable temperaments are good breeding prospects. An aggressive, hyperactive, or shy temperament should not be projected into the next generation. Do not inflict on others your own dog's problems.

Type

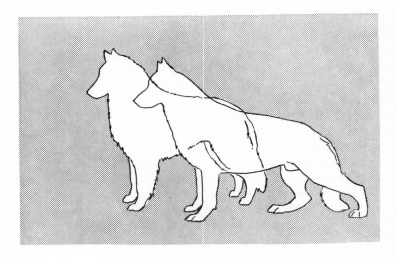

Second to soundness must be type. You should be able to tell a breed of dog by its silhouette. Of course, many laymen do not know what a Lhasa Apso looks like, or are even able to pronounce it. But a knowledgeable person should be able to identify a Bichon Frisé or an English Setter. They should be able to discern a Boxer from a Mastiff and an Akita from a Malamute. Even the uninitiated should be able to tell a Poodle is a Poodle and that an Afghan Hound is an Afghan. What is a Dalmatian without its spots, or a Shar Pei without its wrinkles?

That means whatever gives the breed its characteristic, or "peg," should be apparent in your breeding prospect. A Belgian Sheepdog's ears should stand erect. A Great Pyrenees should be large. A Sheltie should be small—at least in proportion to a Collie. And an Old English Sheepdog should be hairy—and speak with an English accent!

Type is most often apparent in the head or expression.

These qualities need not be the extremes sometimes preferred by connoisseurs of the breeds; however, they should identify the breed. Major deviations from the desired characteristics should not be perpetuated.

Breeders often ask, "What is more important—type or soundness?" The answer is that you can't have type without soundness. That is, a Golden Retriever is not typical of a Golden if it is too crippled to walk or if you cannot trust it with your children.

Play by the Rules—The Standards

The Standard of each breed was formulated to define the ideal. This ideal dog should be able to perform the task for which it was developed. That purpose could be the ability to trot for long periods herding stock, to swim in icy water, to retrieve game, or to function simply as a loving companion.

While you may not care about showing, you should not remain ignorant of the breed Standard. Everything was put into the Standard for a reason. If there is a size maximum, it is possible the breed forefathers discovered that hip dysplasia increased with size, or that larger specimens were too clumsy to do the work for which they were intended. If the Standard calls for a scissors bite, perhaps it was found that teeth wear down with a level bite, or that a bitch with an underbite could not sever the umbilical cord.

Just because your dog is not used for sledding, coaching, or coursing, it does not mean that it no longer needs to be *able* to function. Therefore first-time breeders, as well as those with more experience, should study their Standards again and again, breeding only dogs that comply. The ideal dog has not yet been achieved. When it is, the rest of us can quit.

A copy of your Standard may be obtained from your national breed club. Addresses are available through the American Kennel Club, or from dog magazines.

Mate Selection

If you've decided your bitch is good enough to breed, would you settle for anything less than the best for her? Once it is determined that the bitch is in good health and condition, the search for a mate begins.

In some human societies, it is the girl's parents who select the mate. The males may dance attendance, and occasionally the girl herself may run off without her parent's permission. But good parents want the best for their daughter and are selective—even persnickety—in their choice.

Most breeders probably spend more time choosing their dog's mate than they do their daughter's. That may be because the dogs don't say much when we make the choice.

Since it is the dam's owners who pay for the breeding and who whelp the litter, raise the pups, and place them in good homes, it is the dam's owners who pick the contest winner.

An owner may offer his dog at stud but seldom has the variety of choice bitch owners do. If a male is handsome, a record setter, and highly advertised, his owners may be able to ask a bitch's owner to breed to their male. On the other hand, if he has all of those things going for him, he doesn't have to ask. They'll be waiting in line.

Some breeders make the mistake of starting with a male, then attempting to buy a bitch to match. Even if your male is exceptional, he will not be the right choice for every female in your kennel. The bitch's owners may take their choice of nearly any male in the country. You have the advantage of upgrading through a world of males. Your selection for your bitch should be at least as good as she is.

Good health and temperament on both sides are paramount. The dog should be a good example of the breed. You want Pointer puppies that look like Pointers, not like Whippets. If you need help in choosing a stud, ask experienced professionals. Vets know whether a local stud has sired hearty, happy puppies or progeny suffering major medical or mental problems.

If you're pleased with your bitch, ask her breeders. You thought enough of their opinion to buy her, now ask their advice.

Club members, professional breeders, trainers, and handlers can give suggestions, although they may have personal reasons for recommending or not recommending a stud. Usually, however, people are happy to show off their knowledge of such matters.

A potential breeder should study prospects. Breed books and magazines can help you evaluate what is appropriate for your breed. Watch the stud's get. Do you like what you see? Do *not* settle on a stud because the dog is convenient, cheap, or belongs to a friend. If you wind up with a bunch of puppies that are knock-kneed, hide behind the furniture, are crippled by the age of six months, and sport airplane wings for ears, the friendship may not remain beautiful.

Titles should not be the only consideration. Sometimes, because of luck or finances, unworthy dogs finish championships and good ones don't. Pick a dog for the dog himself and for his progeny. Worth is not in titles but in the flesh.

If you are attempting to breed show-quality pups, your study of the breed must be even more intensive. Faults of the bitch must be compensated for and her attributes allowed to dominate. Remember, what you see may not be what you get (see Chapter 2). And some of the stud's value may be good for other bitches, but not right for yours.

A business kennel must eliminate breeding stock that yields hereditary defects or poor quality. Be honest in your evaluation of stock.

Ethics

Although courtesy is not a requirement of dog breeding, ethical, caring breeders become more successful as their reputation spreads. These are some suggestions for bitch owners.

- Call on the first day of season and make an appointment. Even though the lady in question might not cooperate immediately, the stud owner will have a general idea of timing.
- Have the vet culture your bitch and check for stricture, abnormalities, and season status.
- Inform the stud owner about any idiosyncrasies of the bitch's personality or her cycle.
- Exchange pedigrees.
- When shipping a bitch, call to let the other party know she has embarked or landed safely.
- Present your bitch in good health, with no parasites, and immaculately clean.
- Pay the stud fee promptly.
- If your bitch must stay at the stud's longer than the average three days, offer to pay board expenses.
- Notify the stud owner that your bitch is in whelp and when the due date is. That is not only courteous, but smart. He may have some interested buyers.
- Notify the stud owner when the bitch whelps, and give statistics on the litter: number, sex, color, any abnormalities. Also, inform of a miss.
- Don't blame the stud or, conversely, take all the credit for everything. It takes two to triumph or to flop, as the case may be.
- Don't blame the stud for the size of the litter or the sexes. The sex split is a matter of luck and timing. Litter size is often hereditary.

Here are some suggestions for stud owners.

- Refuse any bitch that is unsound or of very poor quality. Your stud will receive at least fifty percent of the blame for the results.
- The same rules on shipping hold true.
- Ditto on health and cleanliness.
- When the bitch is in your care, she is your responsibility. You must provide good food, attention, security, and medical treatment if necessary.

- An unproven male often stands at stud for a smaller fee than the going rate, or for no fee until the bitch shows in whelp.
- Two breedings forty-eight hours apart should be offered when a male is used rarely, to obtain mature sperm. Since ovulation is so iffy and hard to predict, especially with a maiden, two breedings are often given if the male's calendar allows.
- Although the burden of proof is on the bitch, most stud owners give a return in case of a miss.
- If the breeding is not perfect, e.g., an outside tie (see Chapter 5) or an extremely short tie, rest the dog and try again in a couple of hours, and/or offer another breeding in two days.
- If a breeding cannot be obtained, discuss alternative choices with the bitch owner (see AI and Frequency, in Chapter 5).
- Not at all necessary, but extremely generous, is a return breeding for no fee or a reduced fee in case of a smaller litter or one that does not survive the nursery.
- If a puppy has been contracted in lieu of a stud fee, decide what happens in advance, if there is only one pup—or none.

2. A MIXED BAG

Genetics

If you've ever bred a litter, you've used the principles of genetics—whether or not you thought about it and whether or not you achieved the desired results. All reproduction involves genetics—from the fleas that plague the dogs, to the dogs, to their masters. So, the more you can learn about practical genetics, the more predictable (or at least *explicable*) your breeding results will be. It even helps you understand your own kids!

"Genetics" comes from the word *genes*, the units of heredity we all carry inside our body cells. Each dog acquires, at the moment of conception, the genes that decide not only what he'll look like and much of how he'll act, but also what he'll be capable of producing in *his* offspring. Literally, that means one breeding is responsible for the future.

It is hard to understand why the dog may *look* one way but *produce* pups that appear quite different. To understand this and use it to your advantage, you must learn how genes work.

Genes/Chromosomes

Genes are submicroscopic particles, but imagine they are objects you can see and hold. In the body hundreds of genes are attached in a long string called a *chromosome*. Visualize genes as beads of different sizes strung together.

Even though scientists don't know where all genes on the chromosomes fit, we do know the order (site) is always the same and predictable. Pretend that on this imaginary chromosome, gene (1) controls eye color, genes (2), (3), and (4) have to do with head shape and size, (5) and (6) affect tail shape and placement, (7) decides coat color, (8) is coat texture, and (9), (10), (11), and (12) control temperament. To act, genes must occur in pairs, so you'll have to picture a second string of beads to go with the first.

Thus, chromosomes, as well as genes, always occur in pairs. For instance, in gene pair (8), which controls coat texture, the larger bead causes wire coats and the smaller bead is for smooth coats.

Dominant/Recessive

Unlike in football, where the faster or the smarter sometimes wins, here the larger bead *always* wins. A gene represented by a large bead is called a *dominant* gene and the one that's a small bead is called a *recessive* gene. Thus wire coats are dominant and smooth coats are recessive to wire.

If a Dachshund inherits the gene pair (8) 00, of course, he'll be a wire coat. If he acquires the pair (8) 0o, he'll also be a wire, because the wire gene (large bead) dominates or wins over the smooth gene (small bead). Only if Moxie the Dachsie inherits the gene pair (8) oo (double recessive, or two small beads), would he be a smooth coat.

Substitute a capital letter for a large bead and a small letter for a small bead, and you can talk like a geneticist! Thus, if the gene pair at site *(locus)* number (8) is for wire versus smooth coat, use *W* for the large bead and *w* for the small bead. Again, the pairs *WW* and

Ww would both be wire coats and *ww* would be smooth.

Try the following to see if you understand:

Black *B* is dominant over liver *b:* If a Flat-Coated Retriever inherits the genes *bb*, what color is he? Answer: liver.

Self-color (solid color) *S* is dominant over spotted *s:* If a German Shorthair inherits *Ss*, what color pattern is he? Answer: solid color.

Homozygous/Heterozygous

When both genes in a pair are the same, either dominant or recessive, we say the dog is *homozygous* (pure) for that trait or character. He must pass this characteristic to his progeny. If the genes in a pair are different, he's *heterozygous* (carries a recessive) for that trait, and could pass either the recessive or the dominant gene to his offspring.

Simple genes are one pair controlling one trait. Other simple genes on our imaginary chromosome would be at locus (1) and locus (7).

Eye color is produced by (1). If dark eyes are dominant over light eyes, Moxie would have the preferred dark eyes. He is heterozygous for that trait, that is, he has one dominant and one recessive.

Locus (7) would be sable (red) color (dominant) vs. black and tan (recessive). Since Moxie has two small beads (homozygous recessive), he is a black/tan.

Additive Genes

Complex traits such as shoulder angulation, gait, hip structure, or hunting ability are controlled by several gene pairs that act together to produce the visible result. These are *additive* genes. If good shoulder assembly is dominant over poor structure, and there are seven pairs of genes that control the shoulder formation, fourteen dominants would be a perfect shoulder—and fourteen recessives would be the pits.

Most dogs land somewhere in between. The more dominants they inherit, the better shoulder they exhibit. In most additive gene groups, dominants yield Mother Nature's desired result.

Looking again at Moxie and the six possible genes for head shape, his five dominants would create a classy head. With only two out of four dominants for tail set, he would be average on that end.

Five of the eight temperament genes are recessives, which makes him surly with other dogs. Obviously, that could be improved.

This lesson started with beads and had a chromosome pair that looked like this:

Locus   1 2 3 4 5 6 7 8 9 10 11 12
O-o-O-O-O-o-o-O-O- O - o - o
o-O-O-O-o-O-o-o-o- o - O - o

If we substitute letters, we end up with this configuration:

E-h-H-H-T-t-a-W-P-P-p-p
e-H-H-H-t-T-a-w-p-p-P-p

Once we know that *Ee* is eye color, *HHHHHh* stands for head, *TTtt* is tail, aa is black and tan, *Ww* is wire coat, and *PPPppppp* is for personality, you can figure out what Moxie looks like.

Moxie the Dachsie, with dark eyes, lovely head, steep croup, black and tan, wire coat, and peevish temperament:

Knowing this helps you as a breeder in two ways. First, you're now equipped to learn more about genetics, especially in your breed. You're armed with the knowledge and the language of genetics. Second, you can analyze the reverse of the above (which is the way dog owners have to do it): Start with the dog and try to sketch out his genetic configuration.

By studying sources, you can distinguish the single (simple) gene patterns in your breed. The multiple (additive) genes will be mostly guesswork, but you can keep in mind that the harder a trait is to modify from one generation to the next, the more genes are involved. For example, length, texture, and color of coat are relatively easy things to change, and they all involve single or few genes.

On the other hand, traits like herding ability, head type, and rear angulation don't change much from generation to generation, and involve many genes. They are harder to improve upon than simple gene traits.

Mode of Inheritance

While the imaginary chromosome had twelve pairs of genes, in reality there are many hundreds of genes on each chromosome. Dogs have thirty-nine *pairs* of chromosomes—seventy-eight total. People have forty-eight pairs. Wolves have seventy-eight, cattle sixty, cats thirty-eight. Birds are varied, which is why you don't see mutt-birds or bird-dogs! Donkeys have sixty-two and horses sixty-four. Their offspring, the mule, has sixty-three and is sterile, which is Mother Nature's way of getting back at us when we mess around with her laws and cross-breed closely related species.

Again, each species has a different number of chromosome pairs. This is why you cannot cross-breed very dissimilar species, such as tigers and pythons or dogs and cats, even in a laboratory. When the chromosomes line up, there is no match. Thus they can't give the message to produce offspring.

When the body prepares for reproduction, the chromosome pairs split up; only *one chromosome, containing half of each gene pair,* ends up in each egg or sperm. (Isn't that a miracle?)

In our example, half of Moxie's sperm cells would contain *E-h-H-H-T-t-a-W-P-P-p-p* and half would have the chromosome *e-H-H-H-t-T-a-w-p-p-P-p.*

But since there are thirty-nine pairs in real dogs, the probabilities become innumerable. Try another analogy: Imagine chromosomes as blocks of different shapes. Our "animal" has six pairs of chromosomes—two stars, two squares, two triangles, two circles, two rectangles, and two half-moons. One of each pair is white and one is black.

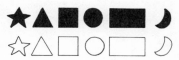

Put all these blocks in a bag. Reach in without looking and pluck out one of each shape. The first round you may end up with

☆ △ □ ● ■ ☾   in your hand and   ★ ▲ ■ ○

□ ☾   left in the bag. The next try may result in   ☆ ▲ ■

○ □ ☾   in the hand and   ★ △ □ ● ■ ☾   in the bag. In fact, mathematically, there are 128 different combinations that could occur by chance, which is why you sometimes wind up holding the bag!

This same chance combination of the chromosome pairs arises in the production of sperm and eggs. This explains why repeat breedings of successes can be disasters.

With thirty-nine pairs in the bag, several million combinations are possible. So it becomes evident why it's hard to produce a carbon copy.

Breeding Roxie the Dachsie

Go back to Moxie and examine the possibilities with just one chromosome pair. Half of his sperm contain the chromosome *E-h-H-H-T-t-a-W-P-P-p-p* and the other half *e-H-H-H-t-T-a-w-p-p-P-p.* Suppose Moxie finished his Championship and is much admired for his typey head. If you had a sable wire Dachsie female, Roxie, with good temperament and good tail set, but you wanted to improve her head quality and eye color, you might choose this male.

Roxie's chromosome pair is something like this:

e-H-h-h-T-T-A-W-p-P-P-P
e-h-H-h-T-t-A-w-P-P-P-p.

Thus *ee* results in light eye; only two *H*'s makes for poor head type; three *T*'s is above-average tail set. *AA* makes her sable; *Ww*, wire, and the six *P*'s generate her friendly, outgoing temperament.

Half her egg cells, when the pairs split, would contain the chromosome *e-H-h-h-T-T-A-W-p-P-P-P*, and the other half would carry *e-h-H-h-T-t-A-w-P-P-P-p*.

Fertilization

Breeding is accomplished—that was easy!—and fertilization transpires. When the sperm containing the thirty-nine single chromosomes unites with the egg, also containing thirty-nine single chromosomes, each chromosome lines up with its corresponding pair. *Voilà!* We now have seventy-eight again. These newly paired chromosomes with their thousands of genes tell each new cell how to develop.

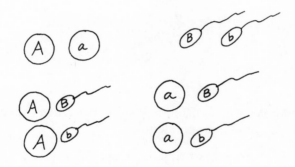

Moxie and Roxie have two kinds of eggs and two kinds of sperm between them. How many combinations could you see in the pups? There are four possible pairings: Sperm *a* with egg *a*, sperm *a* with egg *b*. Sperm *b* with egg *a* and sperm *b* with egg *b*. The law of averages says that twenty-five percent of the pups would have sperm *a*/egg *a*, twenty-five percent would have sperm a/egg b, twenty-five percent sperm *b*/egg *a*, and twenty-five percent sperm *b*/egg b.

Probabilities are accurate only with large numbers—in the hundreds. In a litter of six or seven, it could work out that all sperm *a* reach their goal first and fertilize the *a* and *b* eggs. But in the overall view, assume that one of each combination appears in every four pups. So a litter of four might include:

Pup 1   E-h-H-H-T-t -a-W-P-P-p-p
e-H-h-h- T-T-A-W-p-P-P-P

Mopsy the Dachsie, with dark eye, average head, good tail set, sable, wire, good temperament.

Pup 2   E-h-H-H-T-t- a-W-P-P-p-p
e-h-H-h- T-t-A-w-P-P-P-p

Foxy the Dachsie, with dark eye, average head, average tail set, sable, wire, good temperament.

Pup 3   e-H-H-H-t-T- a-w-p-p-P-p
e-H-h- h-T-T-A-W-p-P-P-P

Flopsie the Dachsie, with light eye, good head, good tail set, sable, wire, average temperament.

Pup 4 e-H-H-H-t-T-a- w-p-p-P-p
e-h- H-h- T-t- A-w- P-P-P-p

Joe the Dachsie, with light eye, good head, average tail set, sable, smooth, average temperament.

Now, be honest—did you improve on your female? Did you eliminate Moxie's faults?

Phenotype/Genotype

Moxie's dark eyes didn't dominate. Why? Because, he is heterozygous for this trait (one dominant and one recessive). The *phenotype* is the characteristic Moxie shows on the outside, the dark eyes. This is versus the *genotype*, the configuration of genes he has for that trait (one dominant dark-eyed gene and one recessive light-eyed gene).

Breeders often say, "He carries the light-eyed recessive," or, "He is a carrier of light eyes." Or, the reverse, "He is free of light eyes."

If he had been a homozygous dominant for dark eyes *EE*, he would have looked the same (dark eye), thus his phenotype would be the same. But his genotype would have been different, double dominant, and all his pups would have been dark eyed, even from our *ee* female.

How about heads, which you really wanted to improve? All four pups had a better head than Mom, but no one was as nice as Dad. Remember, that the more genes involved in the trait, the harder it is to improve. Taking one of the pups with a good head from this litter and breeding it to another superheaded mate would improve head type even more. This time, your outcome was two good heads that could compete in the show ring.

Tail sets were average to good. All of our sample pups have average to above-average temperaments, so they'll fit happily into their new homes.

You know the color genotype of our male, because black/tan is recessive *aa*. After seeing that all the pups are sable out of our sable female, we can be fairly certain of her genotype, a homozygous dominant for sable, *AA*. The result is all sable pups, carrying the black/tan recessive, *Aa*.

Notice you produced one smooth pup out of four from two wire parents. You know the parents both must carry the smooth recessive. It takes two recessives *ww* to produce the smooth and one gene from our pups' pair comes from each parent. Each parent has to have at least one *W* to be wire-coated, so you can figure that both parents are the genotype *Ww*.

Test Breeding

Since so many of the medically dangerous traits that crop up from time to time are recessive, it is probably wise to reemphasize them. Traits like general PRA, hemolytic anemia, cleft palate, dwarfism, umbilical hernia, and others are all known recessives. The same is true of show faults such as long coats in German Shepherds, smooth coats in German Wirehair Pointers, and particolor Boston Terriers.

If your Malamute stud produces 40 (or 140) pups without a dwarf and the bitches he is bred to don't carry the recessive, you'll never see one. But if the twelfth litter contains a dwarf, we *know* he has carried the recessive for dwarfism all along. We also *know* that fifty percent of all the other pups he has produced up until now are carriers of dwarfism. (Whoops!) You can't just blame the bitch of that twelfth litter, although she is also a carrier. A known recessive *has to come from both.* In order to avoid such surprises, do your homework and be aware of recessives, especially those with health aspects, carried in your breed.

You have no way of knowing about a recessive trait except by test breeding. "Proving" your dog carries (or is free of) a recessive is accomplished by breeding your dog to one that is homozygous for that characteristic. Another accepted alternative in making the claim is after breeding to three *known* carriers, without producing it. An educated guess, however, of whether the dog carries the recessive can be made by studying his ancestors and their progeny.

Sex-Linked

One chromosome pair is distinct from the others. The two in the female's pair are alike and called the *XX* pair. But in the male, one chromosome of his twosome is shorter than the other, as if half of the beads were removed from one string. His is called the *XY* pair. When the female's chromosomes split apart, all of her eggs contain an *X* chromosome—since that's all she's got. But each sperm contains either an *X* or a stubby *Y* chromosome. At conception, the *X* egg can unite with an *X* sperm to produce a female pup (*XX*), or a *Y* sperm to produce a male (*XY*). Thus it's the male that determines sex, and it averages a fifty-fifty outcome.

The genes on this pair include those that produce sex organs and hormones, secondary sex characteristics, mothering and mating behavior—all the things that make boys different from girls. But there are many other genes on this chromosome pair, and these can produce traits known as "sex-linked."

Generalized myopathy and hemophilia A are two examples of sex-linked recessives that occur in dogs. Others can be found in the Glossary.

When studying dogs, we know that a single recessive never expresses itself on the other chromosomes, since it is overpowered by its paired dominant. But on the male's *XY* chromosomes, the genes on the long end of the *X have no opposing pair* on the shortened *Y.* Single recessives that occur here express themselves without a matching pair. Thus a recessive sex-linked trait (that is, one that occurs on the *X* chromosome) can express itself in the male offspring even though only one parent passed it to him. Recessives on all other chromosomes must come from both parents to be expressed.

Hemophilia is represented by *h* and a normal, nonbleeder is *H*. A female theoretically could be *HH* (normal/noncarrier), *Hh* (normal/carrier), or *hh* (bleeder). Since there is no pair in the male, there is no carrier state. An *HH* female can *only* produce normal males (*H*) since she is the only one giving *X* chromosomes to her sons. Even bred to a bleeder male (*h*), her male pups would be normal (*H*) and all her females would be normal carriers (*Hh*). An *Hh* (carrier) female bred to an *H* (normal) male could produce *HH* (normal) and *Hh* (normal/carrier) females, and *H* (normal) and *h* (bleeder) males. Only in the laboratory situation of a carrier female (*Hh*) being bred to a bleeder male (*h*) would you expect both male (*h*) and female (*hh*) hemophiliacs as well as carrier females (*Hh*) and normal males (*H*).

Thus, the sex-linked traits are carried by the female and mainly expressed in the males. Don't forget there are thirty-eight *other* pairs at work at the same time. Before you despair, read on about breeding programs.

Natural Evolution

If you're using genetics the way you should, trying to produce better specimens that will breed true, you are attempting to change the genetic pattern of the breed. Did you ever wonder why, even in a puppy-mill situation where the breeding is indiscriminate, the products still look like dogs, still have their eyes and ears and legs in the right number and places? Even a poor example of a Basenji still looks more like a Basenji than a Bloodhound or a Borzoi.

A million years' natural selection by survival of the fittest as well as hundreds of years' prudent artificial selection by breeders rest behind your dog's genetic makeup. Selection created the majority of gene pairs as homozygous.

Evolution provided the correct gene pairs for teeth, eyes, four well-muscled legs, adequate coat protection, and other physical and mental traits vital for survival.

A few recessives still lurked in the gene pool. In the wild, defective whelps die, not thrive. Even if the recessive matched with another to produce an undesirable feature (e.g., short coats in an Arctic climate), the resulting offspring would die. Even a neutral trait such as color variation wouldn't breed true, because it is a recessive.

It is clear why the majority of desirable traits are dominant. But Mother Nature provides a small percentage of heterozygous genes, allowing for adaptation and evolution.

An example of this would be the adaptation of a population of smooth-coated dogs living in a warm climate that slowly becomes colder over the centuries. Eventually, the smooth-coated dogs would perish. However, a few long-coated specimens could be produced through recessive genes. Since they would be more vigorous and more able to thrive in the frigid clime, the long-coats would lead their packs and multiply.

Over time, more and more long-coats would exist and the smooths would degenerate, until finally all the dogs would be homozygous for long coats. That is essentially what happened with the heavy-coated Afghan in the cold elevations of Afghanistan, while his finer-coated cousins, the Greyhounds and Salukis, thrived in the hot desert regions.

Selective Evolution

By actively selecting breeding partners, man accomplishes the same effects as nature, but manages in less time. Breeders began by opting for superior attributes, then went on breeding to fix the new characteristics. Without realizing it, early breeders were tinkering with the small percentage of heterozygous traits present and making them homozygous, artificially prodding evolution.

Early dogs, upon scenting prey, immediately leaped, seized, and killed it. Notably, a few dogs crouched, hesitating briefly before springing at prey. While not of value in the wild, this trait was an immense help in allowing hunters (long before the days of gunpowder) time to throw their nets and capture several birds.

The breeding of dogs with this quality developed "setting" breeds, which freeze into the classic point upon scent or sight of game and hold it for long periods. This trait is now essentially fixed and homozygous where it once was an oddity.

Breeders achieved homozygous traits over the years, with preferred color patterns, coat qualities, distinctive head and body types, temperaments, and other working qualities.

Great Expectations

Before you select a male, make a list of your bitch's good traits and those you'd like to see improved. Study books and photos, watch dog shows, evaluate litters, and ask questions. Seek advice from several people whose dog knowledge you respect. Forestall an attack of a disease peculiar to dog breeders. When "kennel blindness" strikes, all dogs with a certain kennel name on them appear more beautiful and less faulty than dogs of other bloodlines.

If your female has several areas that need improving, you'll probably choose an *OUTCROSS* mating. This means there'll be no common ancestor in the pedigrees—at least in the preceding three or four generations.

In selecting a male for your outcross, you should designate one that is particularly strong in the areas that your bitch lacks. Try to see that he also *produces* those traits. If you need topline and rear angles, try to find a male strong in those aspects. If you find most of the pups he has produced have no better topline and rear angles than your bitch, the male probably has a worse genotype than phenotype. You'd better keep looking.

Don't let big wins and advertising hype sway you. All the ribbons in the world can't guarantee or change genotype.

With a bit more experience and a female who doesn't have too many faults, you may want to try to establish a line. This is a strain that breeds true and is consistently stamped with the traits and characteristics you find desirable.

This will, of course, take many generations, and can only be done through *LINEBREEDING* and/or *INBREEDING*. These established breeding tools differ only in degree of intensity. Select a mate who has ancestors in common with your female; how many times and how close names appear in the pedigree determine whether the term used is "linebreeding" or "inbreeding."

Close breeding of similar animals is used to "set" traits—that is, we try to make the offspring homozygous for the desirable characteristics and thus accelerate evolution. Naturally, homozygous animals tend to be prepotent and produce animals that look like themselves. Genetically, their genotypes and phenotypes are close to being the same.

It matters very little that your girl's pedigree is full of Champions if she is faulty herself. The Dachshund family mentioned earlier in this chapter proved that two fairly nice dogs may not produce superstars. Pedigrees are only as good as the dogs that represent them, just as a fine family may have skeletons rattling.

When the long-awaited litter arrives, select the female pup that carries the strongest attributes you want. She will be the foundation for your next generation.

A good breeding program takes planning, fortitude, hard work, patience, and a bit of luck. That all-Champion litter surely won't come the first time, and maybe not the tenth, but intelligent use of these genetic principles should bring you closer to your goal each time.

Outcrossing

Uninformed people assume that outcrossing is the safest method of breeding. That is not necessarily true: It is not the method that makes a pairing good, but the individuals involved. For instance, the most extreme example of outcrossing is mongrels.

Since it is difficult to obtain two dogs that do not have any common ancestor, (ten generations contain 2,046 names), outcrossing is considered to be two dogs having no common ancestor in three or four generations. The first three generations have the greatest effect, since the influence is well diluted by the fourth generation.

The main reason for outcrossing from familiar lines is to introduce a much-needed characteristic. If you have consistently been producing good conformation, health, and temperament but have been losing pigment, a prepotent but unrelated dog with an ancestry of good pigment should be found. It is important the dog have a good *background* of the desired attribute. He should not be a fluke. Of course, to maintain the qualities already secure in your lines, the dog with good pigment should have adequate producing ability in other areas as well.

Outcrossing prospers best when you choose partners that have been linebred themselves, although they are not related to each other. In this instance, there can be some expectation of results. The representatives should be first-rate if the efforts of past breedings are not to be lessened.

Another method of reaching the same goal is to use dogs from different lines, although with similar traits. In other words, two completely unrelated lines can produce plush, gorgeous coats. One side might be dominant in producing excellent attitude, but needs better backs. The other side could carry iron backs, but have a ho-hum attitude. Outcrossing can reintroduce energy and vigor.

Linebreeding

Linebreeding is the method most commonly used by novice and veteran breeders alike. It does no good—in fact, it may be harmful—to linebreed on a mediocre dog.

This is a safe method for the novice, if he concentrates on the bloodlines of a quality dog that produces like quality. The technique is valuable to the professional when used to enhance an attribute for a kennel.

In selecting a male for linebreeding, it is doubly important to look at the dog himself and at his production record, and not just the fact he's in the pedigree. If, for example, you want to breed back to your bitch's grandfather, Famous CH Jake, you'd better make certain that her tendency for long loin and light eyes didn't come from him. If it did, you'd be fixing those poor qualities in the line permanently, rather than the gorgeous coat and good movement you wanted.

It might be better to go to the grandfather on the other side, Good Old Plain Joe, even though he's not a champion, especially if you've seen him throw dark eyes and short bodies. Or perhaps there is a son of Famous CH Jake who better produces what you want.

Linebreeding on a good dog with a superior shoulder, for instance, can build a sound foundation for shoulders. However, the breeder must not become so engrossed in producing superior shoulders—or rears or coats—that he loses sight of the total dog.

No matter what manner of breeding is used, the whole dog must be considered. If the line producing movement also carries a gene for a missing tooth, the fault will be set in as firmly as the attribute.

The procedure of linebreeding may not reach a goal as quickly as inbreeding, but is less liable to produce flawed animals.

All in the Family

Whenever the uninformed see a dog with problems, they are inclined to blame it on inbreeding. Inbreeding, technically, is breeding to a close relative, for example, mother to son, daughter to father, sister to brother, half sister to half brother. Inbreeding was instrumental in establishing new breeds.

The problem lies not with inbreeding itself, but with the dogs used. Naturally, when breeding closely all defects are doubled, as are the assets. If you elect to inbreed you must verify that the breeding partners offer no severe faults and possess major attributes and few minor flaws. In other words, they should be paragons of virtue.

In addition, you must expect to see whatever problems exist in the line surface and be prepared to deal with them in whatever manner you have chosen. A kennel that chooses inbreeding should be familiar with the entire pedigree *and* the problems associated with the dogs in those lines. Inbreeding is not for the timid or the novice.

Selectors of this mode should be aware that continued inbreeding may decrease size and fertility. Inbreeding for several generations may also cement problems and make them difficult to eradicate. The wise breeder studies his dogs and utilizes the appropriate method. A blending of all three methods—linebreeding, inbreeding, and outcrossing—when needed is the breeding program practiced by successful kennels.

Inbreeding is a valuable tool when used to establish sterling quality. It is also the fastest way to bring recessives to the forefront and eliminate undesirable characteristics.

Therefore, nutsy dogs are not likely to be produced via inbreeding—unless two nutsy relatives are bred. A wiser choice, by far, would be two near-perfect individuals. Inbred dogs are prepotent in producing their own type—even if absolutely awful. Thus inbred litters *must* be carefully culled and the best retained.

Most puppies from an inbred litter are similar to those produced by the other methods. But there is more probability of one or two animals on each extreme end of the scale.

One form of inbreeding is *backcrossing,* which means finding an outstanding male, breeding that male to his best daughter (or his dam, if his dam is superb), taking the best female in that litter and breeding back to said male, and so on.

Naturally, any system should be discontinued or changed once flaws develop or threaten the advantages gained. It is hoped you have noted a consistency in the three methods of breeding. That is, the dogs chosen, whatever the method, should be healthy, sound, and quality examples of the breed.

The world doesn't need more dogs. If you are going to breed dogs, consider it an art form. Use your knowledge of the gene pool to produce superior dogs. You know if you breed a Bedlington to a Bedlington, you'll get Bedlingtons. This is not sufficient to satisfy the true dog connoisseur. The challenge must be to produce dogs a little sounder, a little more beautiful, a little . . . better.

3.   *BUILDING THE FUTURE*

Good Health

No bitch or stud should be bred unless it is in peak condition. If the bitch is infested with worms, severely under- or overweight, or recovering from a serious illness or surgery, she should not be bred until she has had time to regain health. Serious consideration should be given to the breeding partner for months in advance. Be sure the bitch is in optimum health. A prepared breeder keeps an eye on his future at all times, and that means keeping an eye on the future mother.

Extra! Extra!

Feeding and maintaining a healthy brood matron or stud dog does not mean stuffing them with the fad of the moment—extra protein, extra iron, extra vitamins, extra food, and extra extras.

It does mean feeding a first-rate dog food, a balanced diet, and keeping dogs muscular and in prime weight. A stud or brood bitch should not be over- or underweight. Overweight bitches may not conceive at all, or may develop problems during pregnancy or whelping. They should be lean, if not a perfect "ten."

Overfeeding and too many extras cause a dog to become sluggish. Breeding efficiency diminishes. No love handles for your dogs!

Veterinarians state that oversupplementation of vitamins, even through natural food, increases puppy mortality.

Inoculations

The dam's own immunity ensures the pups': The dam passes on her immunity through the colostrum, the first milk. If the dam is not up-to-date on her inoculations, the pups are susceptible to disease. Nothing from nothing is nothing.

Bring the dam to the veterinarian before she is due in season for a premarital exam, including current immunizations. If her shots fall due during pregnancy or while nursing, it is better to give them early to ensure high immunity. It is not advisable to inoculate bitches in whelp, and it is preferable to do so before the season. Any little thing can make a season go "off," particularly when you—and the stud—are waiting.

Although rabies is not a disease that young pups are liable to catch, airborne and other infectious viruses are extremely debilitating or fatal if pups catch them. It is most important that all dogs, particularly dams and puppies, be inoculated against parvo virus and distemper.

Keep in touch with your vet about the latest vaccines to ascertain that your bitch has all the protection available for herself and her brood. Parainfluenza, hepatitis, and leptospirosis vaccines are usually incorporated into the distemper immunization. Laboratories are currently working on perfecting a vaccine for corona virus as well.

Worming

Would you dream of spending a honeymoon with a third party? It sure puts a damper on the fun. To avoid uninvited guests crashing the affair, the bitch should have her stool checked for evidence of parasites before she is bred.

If the test is positive, your bitch should be wormed prior to breeding. Most deworming medications are toxic and are not advisable during pregnancy.

Nevertheless, many puppies are born with roundworm infestation. This is due to the larvae which lie dormant in the dam and reactivate during pregnancy. At that point they enter the bloodstream and thus the fetuses. Parasites may also be transmitted while nursing, which proves that all is not pure, even in mother's milk.

If the mother is infested, her condition is not A-one. Pregnancy and lactation will weaken her further. Thus, the pups would not be as robust as they would with a healthy mother, and these weakened pups soon become infested themselves.

Of course, keeping a stud dog currently inoculated and worm-free is important as well. His health is advantageous to himself and his owner, ensuring his producing ability.

If heartworm is a problem in your area, give your dogs an annual blood test to determine if they are clear, followed by administering the preventative during the danger season.

Routine Tests

Every stud dog and brood bitch should be examined for overall sparkling good health. The veterinary exam can include X rays, a culture to diagnose vaginal or uterine infections, various tests, stool specimen, and a heartworm exam. The vet gives booster shots, listens to the heart, takes the temperature, and examines the genitals for malformation.

An internal examination of the bitch shows if there is a fibrous stricture or narrow pelvis. A sperm count may be taken on males.

A brucellosis test should be run and general sturdiness of body confirmed. Any hereditary breed defects, such as in the eyes, elbow, or patella, should be determined at this time. (See Appendix 1, Breed Specifics and Predispositions.)

If a juvenile vagina is detected, artificial insemination (AI) might be substituted for a natural mating. In many of these cases, whelping follows normally, and a subsequent litter is bred via the time-honored method.

A bitch should be free of any illness, no matter how minor. Breeding a bitch that is in poor shape can only be detrimental to the bitch herself and ultimately to the unborn pups. Hereditary diseases or abnormalities should be avoided in either parent.

Stricture

The premarital checkup should include an internal examination for a vaginal stricture. This stricture is a tough ring at the end of the vaginal canal that an aggressive stud can sometimes tear. It might have to be stretched by a veterinarian. Veteran breeders may be able to obtain the same results, using sterile gloves and petroleum jelly. Occasionally, it is necessary to surgically sever the band. By whatever method, it is painful to the bitch and can put her off from the breeding. However, breeding should take place shortly after surgery, so that scar adhesions do not prevent a later mating.

AI can be performed, if necessary, on a bitch with a stricture. Once pregnancy is accomplished, the ring does not interfere with delivery. A vaginal stricture is often the reason for an "outside tie" (see Outside Tie, in Chapter 5).

Canine Brucellosis

A bitch should be tested for brucellosis before each breeding, and a stud tested once or twice a year, depending on the frequency of use. Smart owners require a clear test result.

Brucellosis is discovered through a blood test. It is convenient to conduct it in conjunction with the annual heartworm exam. Results are obtained quickly in the vet's office. In-office tests occasionally show a false positive. Don't panic yet, but follow up with a specific test run by a state university or private lab.

If the diagnosis is positive, the dog should be isolated and not mated while suspect. Called "canine VD" because the disease is transmitted mainly through sexual contact, brucellosis became widespread around 1962. The disease is very infectious.

In active cases the bacteria is present in vaginal discharge, urine, and fetal fluids. Due to habitual licking and sniffing, the disease is disseminated throughout a kennel and can sterilize all inhabitants. An eruption of brucellosis in a breeding kennel is tragic, since the only way to overcome it is to eliminate all positive dogs, isolating others until a safe period is past—and then preferably move to new promises.

An infected bitch suffers spontaneous abortion around the seventh week of pregnancy. In some instances, pups are carried to term, but are either stillborn or succumb shortly.

Although the disease is not fatal to adults, treatment is not always successful and most adults become sterile. The best prevention is to demand proof of health from the stud's owners.

Bitches usually have a discharge, and males suffer painful swelling of the testicles. Eventually, testicles can atrophy. Glands and joints may also swell and ache.

Don't take this disease lightly . . . especially if you have more than one or two dogs.

Heat Cycle

Speaking in averages—which dogs never are any more than their owners—the average small breed first comes into season at about six months and larger breeds usually at ten to fourteen months. Bitches cycle about every six months. Some, however, come in as often as four times a year, or as seldom as once a year (see Appendix 1, Breed Specifics).

Some bitches can be clocked by the calendar. Others vary widely. As long as they are consistent with themselves, there is no need for concern. Make notes of cycles. Waiting until the second or third heat to breed establishes a pattern and facilitates your plans.

The average heat runs twenty-one days. Some bitches show a bloody flow throughout the season, and others fade to pale pink after ten days.

Certain bitches have to be followed with a mop, others must be tested by flashlight and tissue to ascertain whether they are actually in season. Some bitches keep themselves scrupulously clean; others rise and leave a pool of blood. The safest method of detection is to tissue a bitch, particularly if there are males on the premises or a breeding is planned. Watch for enlargement of the vulva, which may precede flow.

Puberty varies due to breed. Small breeds mature sexually earlier than large breeds. Nature has a way of averaging everything. Small breeds reproduce younger and live longer than large breeds—but they also have smaller litters.

The estrous cycle contains four parts: anestrus, proestrus, estrus, and metestrus. Anestrus is the quiet time between heats, lasting three to five months or longer.

Proestrus is the onset of the heat and discharge. The follicles containing the eggs mature over approximately nine days. Most females refuse mating at this time, by whatever methods. Though flirtatious when it comes to actual mating, they discourage males by baring teeth, growling, snapping, and sitting on it. Some eager matrons, however, cooperate at any time. Fertilization cannot occur during proestrus.

During estrus, the female accepts, in fact invites, coitus with a male. The bleeding often decreases and becomes pale in color. The receptive period of four days to a week is when ovulation takes place. Some females become quite shameless and obvious in drawing attention to themselves. They rub against fences separating them from the male, encouraging his advances. They eagerly move (flag) their tails to the side or curl them completely over their backs.

Timeliness can be checked by rubbing the bitch just above the root of her tail. If she flags, she is approaching ovulation—or is a hussy who doesn't care where or when. Toward the end of the season, the discharge becomes brownish.

Metestrus is the stage that readies the uterus for pregnancy. If fertilization doesn't occur, this stage soon reverts to anestrus. A prolonged metestrus (called a false pregnancy) is common. If pregnancy exists, metestrus continues until delivery.

Disruptions in the heat cycle happen through external influences. Cycles often change as bitches age. Sickness or injury can interrupt the cycle, as may extended daylight. Bitches living under the midnight sun often cycle more frequently, and unseasonable warmth brings early heats. Anestrus may be extended postpartum.

Indications of proestrus may include restlessness, frequent urination, or indigestion. Bitches frequently lick themselves and may lavish affection upon owners. Personality changes often accompany this period—moodiness, flightiness, timidity, and irritation with other dogs.

The rampage of hormones within the body sometimes causes physical changes as well. At least one bitch, a Min Pin, lifts her leg during seasons.

The estrus "perfume" is inspiring to males, who can catch a whiff up to three miles from the source. The scent clinging to clothes makes the owner attractive to males as well, creating the embarrassment of sniffing and mounting.

One bitch tends to bring another into cycle. This common chain is a frustration to professional breeders; with several bitches cycling at once, it's impossible to space out litters.

If you wish to investigate a bitch's pattern for future breeding, run smears throughout the season starting by the fourth day. Record her behavior throughout the cycle (see Smears in Chapter 4).

Training the Stud Dog—Mr. Macho

Training a stud dog should begin when he is a youngster. Accustom the male to having his genitals handled. Should the time come when he needs your help—and it will—touching him will not disturb him. A precocious young male should not be discouraged from mounting bitches, but instead should be distracted when the act is not appropriate.

At sexual maturity a male becomes more selective about mounting. Until that time, he is playing and experimenting. He is not discriminating; any bitch—or dog or person—will do. Once experienced, a stud becomes discerning and mounts only bitches in season. In fact, many studs refuse to breed a bitch until the time is "right."

Males often have a creamy discharge. Should the discharge appear abnormal in color or amount, bring him to your vet. The hair around the sheath should be clipped for cleanliness, as well as convenience in breeding.

Break in a novice stud on a mellow matron, so that his first service is pleasant rather than upsetting. A bitch that snaps or screams is intimidating to a stud, as well as to the handlers.

Use a word to coax that will later be his code word, such as "Up," or "Get the girl." Suddenly a look of surprise enters his eyes, and he'll never be the same again.

A young male is extremely impressionable, as demonstrated by the Keeshond who lifted his leg for the first time on a thorn bush and didn't attempt that action again for three months.

If a male misses on three or more consecutive bitches, particularly proven bitches, have a sperm sample checked. The stud owner should keep records of all litters produced, including any defective pups.

Delayed/Early Heats

Those that wait . . . wait . . . and wait. Part of Murphy's Law is that if you are waiting to breed a bitch, her season will be delayed. If you don't wish to breed, your bitch will be one of those that cycle three times a year.

Bitches can come into heat the first time as early as five months. This might not be a fertile heat, but since a puppy should not be bred, care must be taken that she is not "caught." Although it is unlikely at that tender age, a precocious bitch may be receptive to males. The first heat may be "silent" or "dry" (see the section that directly follows).

If her season is abnormally delayed for your breed, a cycle can be induced by following a course of hormonal treatment. The pet owner will probably be overjoyed that the bitch is delaying the inevitable. Breeders who have plans for a bitch in their breeding program prefer to know whether the coy bitch will ever cycle normally. Professional breeders should discuss the treatment with their veterinarian.

The hormonal treatment may kick off routine cycling. The first initiated heat period might not be fertile, but the bitch can be bred on the second season. Treatment with hormones should never be taken lightly.

Sometimes all that is necessary is biding your time. If the family line shows late sexual maturity, don't panic. Remember a Saluki owner who waited patiently for three years for normal cycling to begin.

Silent Heat

Cases of dry or silent heats have been reported. In one instance, an American Staffordshire bitch showed no external signs. Only the stud dog knew for sure.

A Samoyed breeder wrote of a bitch that cycled with a normal season in the fall and a silent season in the spring. Both were fertile.

Split Heat

Occasionally a bitch appears to come into a normal season, but ceases discharging after just a few days. Stress or trauma can cause such an anomaly. Similar cases have been noted during weather changes or extremes, and in bitches who are shipped to the stud.

Although the delay is frustrating, these bitches often come back into season again in a few days. If there is a lapse of a day or two, it is safest to count from the first day of the "first" season. However, if there is a span of several days to weeks, ovulation occurs normally during the "second" heat.

Extended Heat

An extremely long season may indicate hormonal problems. One treatment is megestrol during the season. The use of "birth control" pills to skip a season often helps return the bitch to synch next time.

The bitch should be examined for other irregularities. One of those "you think *you've* got troubles" stories disclosed a Black and Tan Coonhound bitch who remained constantly in season. Cystic follicles were discovered and ruptured during surgery. The bitch proceeded to cycle normally. She was bred six months later and whelped a normal litter.

Cystitis

Cystitis is a bladder infection, more common in females than in males, foreshadowed by frequent urination. There may be bloody urine, a strong fishy odor, or painful urination—for them, not you, unless the frequency causes accidents on the Oriental rug.

Lack of control sometimes accompanies the infection. Dogs with cystitis may have spontaneous loss of urine, such as when sleeping or walking, or may have the sensation of urination without voiding. Victims often lick their genitals and may have a discharge.

A specimen will determine which antibiotic is effective. Catch the urine in a flat pan and transfer it to a clean jar—this is easier than trying to divert the flow at midstream into the jar!

Bitches with a predisposition to cystitis can have flare-ups following or prior to a heat period. Treatment is necessary to prevent kidney infection, as well as for the sake of your rug.

Pyometra

There are two types of this uterine infection. The open cervix form, showing discharge, is more easily treated. The discharge is sticky reddish pus, often appearing after a season or up to three months postpartum. It may be foul smelling. If the dog is pregnant, she will abort.

The closed-cervix type pyometra contains pus sealed within the uterus. The symptoms are increased thirst and urination, fever and tender abdomen, which may be bloated. Vomiting may occur.

Although pyometra once led to certain spaying or death, other treatments for open pyos are now available. Attempts should be made to clear the infection of a valuable producer by flushing the uterus and/or treating with prostaglandin injections.

This disease is most common in bitches over the age of six years, and can be prevented by spaying once the bitch is retired from the breeding program.

Rarely, bitches can suffer chronic uterine infections; one case involved a flare-up every other season. Once discovered to be a pattern, the infection was treated with antibiotics. On the ensuing normal heat, the bitch is fertile and can be bred.

Infertility/Missing

Infertility is displayed by difficulty in reproducing, irregular seasons, misses, or abortions. Another symptom is delivery of puppies that are weak or die.

Lack of nutrition and poor condition are the major causes of infertility. Obesity, age, or administration of steroids or other medications for a lengthy time may interfere with reproduction. Overuse in breeding can result in temporary infertility. Difficulties could also stem from a lack of hormones, congenital abnormalities, or various diseases. When a dog is debilitated, the first thing to lapse is fertility. Summer heat can decrease a male's potency.

Other causes:

- Orchitis (testicle inflammation) caused by injury or infection. The testicles become enlarged, hard and painful.
- Epididymitis, which is an infection obstructing flow of sperm.
- Hormonal imbalance, which can cause testicles to atrophy.
- A sperm-duct blockage, congenital or otherwise, which can be determined by a biopsy and corrected with surgery.
- Streptococcus and other bacteria shown in vaginal or sheath cultures.
- Hypoestrinism, induced by low estrogen, is exhibited by low libido or short, abnormal heats.
- Hypothyroidism generates irregular heats and is diagnosed by a thyroid test from a blood sample.

Some of these conditions are treatable. But it is often difficult to discover the root of the trouble. Whether breeding is worth the extensive examinations and treatments must be considered. Many of these conditions are hereditary.

Before panic sets in, however, the simplest approach to the problem of an unproductive bitch is to find a highly fertile local stud with cooperative owners. Take daily smears from day four. Attempt breedings early. Continue breeding every other day until one or the other quits. In one case, it was the owners who finally called a halt after four breedings—their bitch conceived despite three previous misses.

Infertility and low libido do not necessarily go together. Therefore, a dog or bitch that is not interested might conceive through AI or forced breeding. Perversely, avid breeding partners may not reproduce after an orgy of mating.

A common story is of a bitch that was bred to several carefully selected studs to no avail. But when she chose her own beau, often a kennel mate, the breeding resulted in a litter. Unfortunately, the choice may not only be wrong for her, but the wrong breed.

Sterility

Inability to reproduce might be caused by illness, with temporary or permanent consequences. Sterility can be caused by a high temperature, heat prostration, or infection.

Some causes can be diagnosed by biopsy, or by blood, sperm, and other tests. Of course, sterility might be congenital or due to brucellosis.

Thyroid

Hypothyroidism may cause infertility. Thyroid disease can be hereditary, and must be a consideration when deciding whether to breed. Many breeds have a high incidence.

Symptoms are loss of hair, poor coat, dark skin coloring (especially on the abdomen and groin), thickened skin, lethargy, and weight gain. Reproductive symptoms, which can appear without other signs, are loss of libido and abnormal heat cycle. The first indication may be lack of conception. The veterinarian will run a T-3 or T-4 thyroid test to determine if there is a problem.

The disease is easily treated with oral hormone, but treatment must be maintained for life. The consequences of the disease may be mild or severe. A Golden Retriever showed irregular cycling, with two and a half years between seasons.

Another case, a German Shepherd, suffered complications from skin allergies. Before hypothyroidism was diagnosed, she whelped two normal-sized litters, although always losing several whelps. She regressed to smaller litters, culminating in sterility.

Vaginitis

An infection of the vaginal tract is apt to surface at any time, but is more common during a heat or after a breeding. There is a creamy discharge, which owners might mistake for a heat or pyometra.

If the discharge is off schedule or has pus, a culture should be taken. The culture determines which bacteria is present, so the effective antibiotic can be dispensed. Antibiotic infusions may be suggested.

The infection is lethal to sperm, and breeding can also infect the male. If the bitch receives the infection as a gift from the male during mating, the vaginitis does not preclude conception. The veterinarian should be forewarned that the bitch may be in whelp when attempting to diagnose and treat the infection.

Sperm Test

It is easier to obtain a specimen by using a bitch in season as a tease. The specimen is examined for color, amount, any debris or foreign matter, number and motility of sperm, and whether or not there are live or deformed sperm. The average stud dog has around two hundred million sperm per ejaculate. It's hard to believe misses take place!

4. GOING BY THE BOOK

Breedings

It is advised to withhold food before breeding. Feeding can make the male sluggish or even nauseous during the excitement. If, however, the erotic damsel is residing on the premises, most males tend to go off their feed. Exercise both dogs. The mating act stimulates more than the libido.

Some breeders recommend washing genitals with a disinfectant soap both before and after breeding. Rinse thoroughly as residual soap could be spermicidal. Generally, washing isn't necessary with healthy animals. Trimming long hair surrounding genitals facilitates matters.

The actual mating calls for two dogs and, preferably, two people. One person holds the bitch and keeps her calm, giving her physical assistance in supporting the male's weight. The other person aids the male, guiding him, cheering him on, and assisting him to turn or dismount. This person can also move the bitch's tail to one side if she does not flag. With nervous or inexperienced dogs of large breeds, three people are even better.

Help is always appreciated. A breeder confessed she needed four hands to handle a Staffordshire bitch who was playful to the extent of rolling on the ground and scampering off at inopportune moments.

When breeding a certain English Setter stud, assistance was not simply a luxury, but an absolute requirement—for the dog would only take his fun on the run. His mistress had to be trotted ahead of him, with the stud tearing after her. The same dog who turned his head with boredom at a vamp soliciting on a stance bred with gusto when she took flight. Perhaps he thought he'd miss the boat!

A small bitch can be restrained with a hand under her belly. Larger breeds are supported with a knee under the loin. The knee helps in elevating her, if necessary. Toys are often bred on tables, which is easier on helpers' legs and backs. Many owners leave collars on the dogs, giving themselves something to grab—besides dog—if need be.

If the bitch is violent, she might have to be tranquilized and muzzled or bred by AI (see Chapter 5). At the opposite extreme, a German Shepherd breeder reported her bitch was so relaxed she'd fall asleep as soon as the tie was effected.

When the stud is new at the game, encourage him to sniff and mount by patting the bitch's rump. When he makes an attempt, praise—even if it's in the wrong vicinity. Scoot the bitch around to the right position, and he'll soon find the right place is more fun than the wrong one.

Some dogs are coy and flirty, and they should be allowed time for courtship. Don't rush matters.

If the male becomes overexcited and is tiring himself to no avail, take him away and allow him to urinate. The idea that he might lose out if he doesn't do things right might spur him on to the goal.

Once the tie is accomplished, two people are able to control the dogs from making sudden movements, keep them content, and keep each other company. It gets to be an old and really boring thing watching two dogs carry on. Having two people present means one person can call for help if there is trouble. If nothing else, you might speculate on the future litter while waiting.

The authors recommend that no breeding be unsupervised. However, after several aborted plans, "natural" breedings have been allowed by some veteran breeders under controlled conditions.

Os Penis

The canine penis, unlike other mammals', contains a bone. This means an injury could cause a fracture.

Naturally fractures are painful. This bone obviously cannot be set in a cast or a sling. Care should be taken during breeding.

Cleanliness

It is more pleasant for owners to handle dogs that are clean and odorless. The dogs couldn't care less. Their mate might smell like a lump of very old Limburger cheese and they'd be happy.

The Loving Room

Experienced stud owners advise conducting all breedings in the same location. Most males perform better when everything is familiar and they are alert to expectations.

Breedings are customarily conducted at the home of the male. The reason for this chauvinistic approach is simple. If the male were shipped or delivered to the bitch's residence every time he was bred, some popular studs would spend more time traveling than airline pilots. Also, the male is more dominant on his home turf, and the bitch will submit more readily to his advances away from her territory.

The flooring must be nonskid, a rug or matting, for example. If feet slide at the wrong time, the results would be painful or awkward at the least. The surface should be large enough to save the breeders' knees.

Keep the room quiet and free of distractions—other dogs, kids, puppies, TV sets, extra people—particularly for the novice stud. A Don Juan may achieve a mating in the middle of a parking lot, as breeders have reported, but you should certainly not attempt to break in a youngster in a circus atmosphere. If the breeder wants to take advantage of the time for sex education, he should use two experienced dogs.

Two more pieces of advice: For the comfort of dogs and handlers, do not plan matings for the hottest time of day; and find a place that is free of flies.

The Stud's Kit

Stud owners soon learn to have some equipment available. Even if not needed, it's comforting to know that it is handy and that you will not have to search during an inconvenient time.

Handler comfort should also be considered. A couple of low footstools or similar items will be appreciated during the ties.

Also:

Nonslip floor covering   Cleanup equipment
Petroleum jelly   Pan of water
Sterile gloves   Leash
Ice cubes   Muzzle

Aiding

The stages of the breeding are courtship, mating, and tie. Some males get right down to the nitty gritty without messing around. They consummate the sexual act without any of the amenities, and that's fine—it's normal.

Other males spend several minutes licking, sniffing, pawing, and blowing in ears. They believe in taking it slow and easy, and that's normal, too.

Most develop a routine. One stud may dance around, asking permission before he gets down to business. Another mounts, dismounts, whispers in her ear, resumes his position, and Bingo! Yet a third knows what's happening as he approaches his mating grounds. He enters the room and possesses the bitch before she is even aware of his presence.

The male mounts and thrusts until he hits what he is aiming at. He then picks up momentum and his legs seem to tread water for a minute. He has achieved his purpose, and ejaculation takes place.

There are three parts of the ejaculate. The first is clear and rinses the urinary tract. It is about this time the tie is accomplished by the gland swelling.

The milky second part contains the sperm, and the third portion (clear again) helps drive the sperm toward the waiting ova.

No matter how eager the two are, dogs should never be left alone. Even the most congenial and cooperative dogs may move at the wrong time and injure each other.

If you have trained your dog correctly (see page 39), he will not object to your touching the bitch or him even in the throes of passion. The bitch's head should be held still and her rear in position. A little petroleum jelly helps in a tight spot.

It is a mistake to allow a male to do as he wishes and take the bitch without handling. This is not only poor training, it's unsafe.

If the coupling must be handled by one person, the bitch can be restrained by a hitching-post method. This can be done by tying the bitch with a short lead. When the handler's knee is placed under her groin, she will not be able to pull away. The stud should be well trained, and the handler confident that both dogs will remain calm.

In the event there is no tie, rest the dog for a half hour and try again. Many times the second effort is successful. If not, the attempt may be twenty-four to forty-eight hours early (see Outside Tie, in Chapter 5).

The Tie That Binds

A veterinary assistant recalls the time a client rushed into the office exclaiming that his dogs were stuck together. This is normal, although peculiar to dogs. Once the act is accomplished, no amount of yelling or dousing with water will end it. The tie is caused by a bulb which swells on the penis. At the same time, the vaginal muscles constrict, resulting in the "stuck" dogs.

Ties last from a fraction of a moment to forty-five minutes—or longer (see Extended Ties, in Chapter 5). Usually the range is ten to twenty minutes. Records of a Miniature Schnauzer breeder show variations of successful breedings ranging from no tie to ninety minutes, with an average being five minutes.

During this time, the male may choose to turn, and the handlers should aid him. Hold the bitch still and help the male lift his leg over her back to turn, so they stand butt to butt. Holding the tails of small dogs together when turned helps keep them still. This is the preferred position in the wild, as they can still protect themselves.

They may also stand side by side or lie down. Lift the male down from the bitch's back and help them assume a posture that is comfortable for them and for those assisting the breeding.

The dogs should be kept still, as sudden movement can be painful. If the bitch pulls away, there could be hemorrhage or tissue damage to both. Avoid this by exercising sufficient control over the dogs during breedings. Talk quietly and praise them, holding firmly. Before the separation, many studs lick themselves, anticipating the end of the tie.

Ties are normally boring rather than eventful, but there are exceptions. The first time her Affenpinscher stud fainted during a tie, his owner was alarmed. Now she accepts it with humor. As she said, "He goes out with such a look of delight on his face!"

A tie is not necessary for conception, but does increase the percentages. Once the tie is broken, remove the bitch and crate her for at least half an hour. Do not allow her to urinate. A maiden may have a small amount of fresh bleeding, which is of no concern.

Examine the male to see whether the penis has retracted normally. Occasionally, a tie cannot be accomplished (see Outside Tie, in Chapter 5), and if the bitch moves too soon the male is left exposed. It helps to immerse the penis in a pan of cold water. If left uncovered, the penis dries out and becomes sore.

Give the male water to drink and a treat to eat to thank him for being so cooperative, then let him relieve himself. Nobody ever mentions giving the bitch a treat, but why not? After all, it takes two!

The Serenade—Vocal Breeding

The male is strong and silent once he has his way. The bitch, however, may tell the whole world what this lusty male is doing to her innocence. Some bitches, even matrons, cry and voice their displeasure during the entire process. This can discourage an inexperienced stud, or even the owner.

A maiden often cries during the first penetration, particularly if the breeding is attempted early and she is not sufficiently dilated. Noise does not always reveal pain, for a sophisticated matron sometimes moans and utters little squeaks of pleasure. Unfortunately, this usually occurs about the time the poor old dear is ready to be retired and put out to pasture.

Timing

After the marital decision is resolved and the choice of the groom made, the date is the next determination. Timing is a prime aspect. Owners who have chosen a local dog or are boarding their bitch at the home of the stud are not under as much pressure as those who must ship the bitch or travel to her fiancé.

Many bitches are good indicators of correct timing, arching their backs and "flagging" their tails. Others flag during their whole season, and some old gals move their tail even when not in season.

The vulva "winks," tipping up, inviting a breeding. As the time nears, the vulva becomes pouty and more and more swollen. One owner has described this softening as comparing the firmness of your nose to the softness of your lips.

The male, too, is a good time clock. An experienced swain will not be eager until the aroma signals the time is *now!*

Flirting and inviting the male to play by crouching and wagging her tail, bouncing from place to place, and refusing to stand still are all signs that it is too early. As the season subsides, however, bitches tend to lift a lip at the male's attentions.

In some instances, smears are helpful, but even veterinarians agree that smears must be taken for several days to ascertain progress. The slightest incident can disturb ovulation. Testape® is another indicator to show glucose. Insert the paper into the vagina about two inches. If it turns green, it's a green light. However, false positives have been obtained.

On average, good breeding days are nine through sixteen, with twelve and fourteen being most common for ovulation. However, our survey logged bitches that conceived on day minus four (four days before discharge) to day twenty-four! There may be reasons other than early or late ovulation, for example, dry heat for the first two weeks, or stress or trauma setting back the cycle.

Nothing is certain. Ask the owners of the ten-month-old German Shepherd male who bred a bitch four days before she showed any signs of season, with kennelmates showing no interest. This stud broke all the rules—he was a novice stud younger than average, and bred in the middle of household activity and with no visible season. Naaaaaaa, they said, it'll never take. "Never" resulted in five pups.

Breeders concur that the best way to mate a maiden bitch is to use a stud with cooperative owners. Although the first priority should not be money or distance, a quality local stud is advantageous for first-timers. Good choices may be a young but experienced male, or an older male that is not quite the man-of-the-moment. Stud and owners should have time to be patient with a bashful maiden.

An untried female should be tested daily from the tenth day until she willingly submits, then bred every other day until she refuses, or until the male becomes uninterested. If the breeding does not culminate in a litter, next time try even earlier.

Since the chosen male is not always able to be booked for a long run, and stud owners have other things to do besides dance attendance on your bitch, the breeder does well to study her signals. It is unnecessary to breed more frequently than every other day, for the sperm remain viable for several days and the ova for forty-eight hours. Canine sperm is supposed to live from seven to ten days, but what matters is not the lifespan but the fertility span.

As a bitch ages, ovulation date may change. She should be bred according to her actions or smears, rather than by the calendar.

Smears

Progressive examination of smears can identify the progress and ovulation time during the bitch's heat cycle. While smears need not be routine, it is useful when the bitch must be shipped or she has missed before.

In breeds without tails (no flagging), the smear helps in planning an itinerary. When an AI is to be done, vaginal smears become a necessity to pinpoint the right time.

Your vet will collect a smear from the upper vaginal tract with a sterile swab and examine it under a microscope. After researching the procedure with their vets, some veteran breeders take on this task themselves. A practiced eye is necessary to determine the changes that occur in the physical makeup of the cells during the course of the heat period.

As the season progresses, the cells change from the usual "fried egg" shape, slowly losing their nuclei and becoming wrinkled and folded. Red blood cells can also be seen in the smear, along with

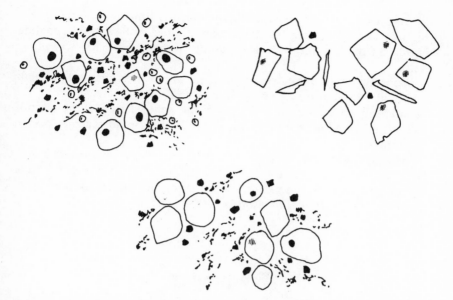

white cells, mucus, and other debris that disappears as ovulation approaches.

Just after ovulation, white cells (neutrophils) reappear in the smear. Examination of one smear can't predict how fast the next stages will ensue. But comparing smears over several days can show when D-Day is close.

Continuing smears after breeding can identify the first day of metestrus. Recent veterinary findings indicate whelping date is *always* fifty-seven days from the first day of metestrus. This could prove helpful if a C-section is planned, if your breed is prone to uterine inertia—or simply if you wish to plan around the date.

Poor Aim

Expect a youngster to try mating the ear, the third rib, or two inches high or low. If a male has been conditioned to having his genitals handled from the time he is a puppy, he should not be shy about help.

Scoot the bitch to the proper position, rather than shoving the male and distracting him. Encourage him to sniff the genitals.

Suddenly he wakes up and aims in the general area. If the bitch is sufficiently swollen, a little boost or guidance should put him on the right track.

Let him try by himself for a time, but if he's just off the bull's-eye, don't let him become tired or discouraged. Aim the vulva a little higher or lower, as the case may demand, and guide the penis into the vulva. Once the connection is made, Eureka!

Frequency

A healthy stud (and there should be no other kind) can be used on an average of two or three times a week, or every other day. Occasionally, he can be used more frequently, but not to the point of exhaustion. Excessive use can lower fertility, and the increased usage becomes futile.

Backup Stud

If standing at regular stud, his diet and protein may be increased in small amounts. Even Champions are rarely in demand by more than two bitches a week. If a dog is extremely popular, it may be wise for

the owner to groom a backup stud in reserve. He can stand in when superstud needs a rest, or when two bitches coincide on fertile days.

Naturally, the bitch's owner should be informed if the preferred stud is unavailable. The stud's owners will ask whether they should bring in the second-string or skip the breeding. If the backup is also a good dog, and particularly if he is related to the favorite, most bitch owners will agree rather than miss the breeding. A good choice for a substitute is a less famous brother, the sire, or a young son.

Frozen Semen

The old saw says you're only appreciated when it's too late. Owners can be sure it's never too late by storing their stud's frozen sperm at approved laboratories, which are advertised in dog publications. Only these labs will do it as is necessary for American Kennel Club (AKC) registration. Freezing and thawing methods can be tricky and can kill the whole attempt.

Not only are shipping costs and danger of animal loss avoided, but timing is simplified by having the same vet reading smears throughout the season. You also eliminate the frustration of the bitch going out of heat due to the stress of traveling.

This is a boon to the owner who lives in a quarantined area. It also gives wider selection to those who do not choose local studs, but cannot or will not travel or ship. One ejaculate can cover four or five bitches.

Back-to-Back Breedings

Successive breedings for a bitch should not be routine. A season's rest is needed between litters. Following back-to-back litters, for whatever reason they occurred, the bitch should be allowed to rest a year before her next breeding.

You might elect to breed a bitch twice in a row if you wish to have her whelp at a more convenient time of year, if she has had infertility problems, or if she has whelped an extremely small litter. However, the bitch should be in tip-top condition. When bred on consecutive seasons more than twice in a row, litters tend to decrease in numbers and the size and vigor of the pups to diminish, so nothing is gained.

The exception may be the bitch who cycles only once a year. It is permissible to breed her on successive seasons since nature has spaced her cycle for a year's interim.

5. DOGS DON'T READ THE BOOK

After endeavoring to mate an uncooperative bitch to a stud, you may wonder how mongrels manage to procreate with such success and enthusiasm.

One German Shorthair Pointer possessed two vaginal tracts. Although you'd think her admirer would be in heaven, it was the opposite for him, as each was too small for penetration. One tract was surgically removed and breeding accomplished by AI. She whelped normally.

Overeager males sometimes have problems during matings when their excitement causes premature ejaculation. The same is true when breeding bitches with small genitals. A Scottie breeder has had success in dilating such bitches. Here's where you'll use the sterile gloves and petroleum jelly in the stud kit.

Sometimes the male's spirit is willing, but the body cannot. There may be a fold of skin over the prepuce, which does not allow the penis to extrude. This may be corrected surgically. Another problem that frustrates young dogs is a flexible penis, which bends like a rubber band when it contacts an immovable force.

Too Much of a Good Thing—Extended Tie

The breeding is finally accomplished, and you've got a tie. You wait patiently, switching from knee to knee. Then not quite so patiently, rubbing your aching back. As the dogs become annoyed with this monotony, you struggle to keep them still so there will be no damage.

The bitch squirms around, whimpers and tries to sit. The male finds part of himself dragged painfully to the floor and screams in objection.

It goes on . . . and on . . . and on. When it extends beyond an hour, everybody's had as much as they can take.

Actually, the phenomenon occurs when two powerful forces are working counteractive to each other. The dogs become anxious to separate, pulling against each other, causing greater discomfort. The vagina grips tighter, and the glans penis stays swollen. So the pressure must be counteracted.

Most breeders questioned hooted in laughter, since the usual frustration is an outside tie or no tie at all. Therefore, everybody is perplexed when they endure a long tie. Among the unlocking methods that have been attempted is an ice pack placed on the male's testicles. As the skin cools, so does the male's ardor.

Another suggestion is to replace the male in the original mounting position. Push on his rear and hold a moment, releasing pressure on the swollen penis. The dog should relax, so the partners are freed.

In one instance, the first package in the freezer was grabbed and frozen corn was substituted for the mundane icebag. In another, the dogs became so bored, they fell asleep and separated.

The oddest thing is male attitude. No sooner does a dog separate from the bitch, than once again he is eager and interested. How fast they forget!

Outside Tie

When you're anxious, it is natural for you to promote a breeding a day or two early. This can result in an outside tie. While outside ties are annoying, the bitch can still become pregnant. An inside tie simply increases the percentages.

To determine if there is a tie, the male's handler should run his hand along the penile shaft to see if the swollen glans is on the outside or the inside of the vulva. If the swelling is on the outside, you can ensure the tie by holding the dogs together for five or ten minutes after ejaculation is completed. This "artificial" tie stops the semen from leaking out. If outside ties are recurrent, the bitch should once again be examined for a stricture.

Some breeds are lethargic, and an outside tie is more often the norm than not. Many who raise athletic breeds do not consider an outside tie a breeding. They back it up with another breeding and/or AI or wait payment until proof of pregnancy. However, for very small (i.e., Maltese), very large (Saints), short legged (Dachshunds), or heavy-bodied breeds (Bulldogs), an outside tie is as common as an inner one. In rare cases, older bitches develop scarring through difficult delivery or prior infection, making a normal internal tie difficult or impossible.

A complication to the outside tie sometimes occurs (Boston Terriers) when the bitch does not release the male up to an hour after swelling diminishes.

If the bitch consistently experiences outside ties without complete penetration, surgery may aid the situation, or breedings may be completed with AI. Many an outside tie becomes a normal breeding forty-eight hours later.

I've Got a Headache—Lack of Female Interest

The bitch who prefers to "sit on it" most commonly has anxious parents who are trying to push her into marriage too soon. If owners are patient, often a day or two changes the little gal's mind, heart, and position.

However, if she persists in being uncooperative, particularly after prior litters, it may be a sign of an abnormal season. Otherwise, she might just be a spoiled mama's (or daddy's) girl.

In the first instance, the season might have to be bypassed and tests run determining the cause. Hormonal treatment sometimes helps.

In the second case, the stud owner would be advised to remove the nervous in-laws. The bitch will calm down when her attention is focused on the male rather than on her hovering owners. Besides, the stud owner can take firm steps to make her stand, using physical restraint, without her owners protesting that their baby is being assaulted.

Sometimes it's best left to the stud. An aggressive dog often takes the situation in hand, so to speak, and shakes the bitch by the nape of the neck, intimating, "Hey! I'm here to do a job. Shape up!" Tranquilizing a nervous, upset bitch is sometimes recommended by veterinarians.

If the bitch continues to complain and smears show ovulation has occurred, the breeding can be accomplished with artificial insemination.

Not Tonight, Dear—Lack of Male Interest

Trust your dog. An experienced stud almost always shows interest if the time is right.

Tantalize an inexperienced male. Kenneling him next to a bitch in season is similar to plopping a pubescent boy on a topless beach on the Riviera. Tease him by bringing in another male to demonstrate. The presence and scent of another male near "his" bitch is often enough to whet the youngster's libido. All dogs should be kept on leash if this is attempted, to avoid an accidental breeding by the wrong stud, or a fight between the two competing males.

If this arouses no interest, let him grow up. He may just be too young, as all mature at different times. A few precocious pups, mostly small breeds, are ready at six months. Some large breeds are not aware until eighteen months to two years. The average dog is ready to embark on a limited breeding program at one year. This is a good age to have a complete physical and initiate the male.

A submissive kennel dog may be intimidated by a bossy bitch. Some gentlemen cease all attention if the bitch growls her dislike or cries in discomfort. A spoiled house pet may refuse to breed. Work up the male's eagerness by removing him for a few minutes.

Dogs with a lack of hormones and very low libido may have to be stimulated by the handler conducting the breeding. The bitch that does not radiate an attractive hormonal scent will not be appealing. Both parties should be examined for abnormalities and hormonal deficiencies if this is a recurrent problem.

However, the main reason for a bored male is poor timing—simply too early or too late in the season. Experienced stud dogs will not touch a bitch until the right day(s). The stud yawns, owners panic, the bitch flirts. He watches everyone pirouetting in front of him, inviting him to participate in the fun. He's thinking, "Not tonight, dear. Maybe tomorrow."

Relax, try again.

Love?

"Love, love, hooray for love!" And who says dogs don't fall in love? Ask any frustrated breeder whose two painstakingly selected prize-winners want *nothing* to do with each other. Along comes a scroungy, nondescript, downright unattractive type and ZAP!

Breeders stand on their heads trying to make the bitch attractive to the male, or trying to convince the bitch that the male they've chosen for her is the best.

Few dogs mate for life. But occasionally a rare Romeo (more often, Juliet) opts to breed to a kennelmate and turns up his nose at the ripe little beauty wiggling her hips and preening in front of him.

The proof of this is the Irish Water Spaniel who ignored the designated bitch in the following tale: "We put her [the hopeful bitch] in the run next to the stud. He kept looking over the top and wailing for a seedy-looking bitch in season on the other side. My bitch stood flagging and flirting but he stood on his hind legs and whined for the other bitch. We tried breeding them. He gave a quick lick and strained to get back to his run. After three days, we used another stud and, while we were busy, someone left a gate open and we came back to find the other two tied. Who says dogs don't fall in love?"

The logical explanation is that the rejected female does not have an attractive hormonal essence about her. Again, timing may be wrong, or a false heat the reason.

Whether love or not, a persistent Saluki raped the object of his affection, though not in season. A twenty-minute tie ensued; a pregnancy did not. In another situation, an English Cocker, stimulated by the bitch next door in heat, bred his kennelmate daughter who was midway between seasons. This breeding did produce five puppies!

Separation from siblings at too young an age and lack of contact with other dogs is destructive to a canine's normal sex life. The dogs simply don't think they're dogs and don't develop natural instincts.

When your Scarlett refuses her Rhett, she may not be just flirtatious or coy, she may be shy and reserved with unfamiliar dogs. One German Shepherd bitch absolutely *refused* to breed to a stranger. If forced, she *would not* conceive. She allowed such privileges only to males of long-standing acquaintance.

If you are determined the breeding *will* take place, and they are just as determined it will *not,* introduce the couple to each other a few days in advance. In humans, distance makes hearts grow fonder, but in dogs, it's proximity.

If nothing else succeeds, breeding may be consummated with artificial insemination.

And next time, use cologne.

"Up Please!"—Size Difference

Dog owners are not all the same size, and neither are their dogs. It's hard to understand how the neighbor's Affenpinscher and Doberman Pinscher could possibly have gotten together. Determination is amazing. When it comes to the breeder's plans, however, it's a different story. The male aims for an hour and is off a foot or two. If it's just poor aim, a little guidance benefits (see Poor Aim, in Chapter 4).

If the male is too short or tall, slip a large catalog or phone book under the rug, or fold the rug. In some breeds, this is common. For instance, the smaller the better is preferred in some Toy breeds, such as Yorkies or Pomeranians. For show purposes, the males are very tiny. The bitches, however, must be of moderate size in order to carry and whelp a litter.

Rig up a platform or ramp for the shorter partner to be elevated. The males quickly become accustomed to such a device, in fact, become ecstatic at its appearance. An ingenious Chihuahua solves his tiny problem himself by climbing on the bitch's hocks, thereby raising his sights.

Some breeders of unwieldy, uncooperative, and/or unmaneuverable breeds build a breeding rack. In fact, one owner was in ecstasy at finding one at an antique sale! They are similar to the stools seen in shoe stores, with straps to tie the bitches down. The fancier models can also be raised or lowered.

If the male is antsy about the contraption, other methods can be substituted. If the bitch is slightly taller, it helps to spread her rear legs. This lowers the objective.

On the other hand, if the target needs to be raised, a hand under the groin area might suffice. More elevation can be gained by placing a knee under the loin, raising and lowering the bitch as necessary. These are all the more reasons why the male should be accustomed to performing at your command.

Unattractive Season

Some seasons are unattractive to males. Whether the problem is lack of hormone, a false season (no ovulation), or other influences is difficult to diagnose.

A heat may show bleeding with no swelling, or swelling with no bleeding—or occasionally both—but the bitch is not alluring. A female might invite attention by standing and flagging or act bored by the whole procedure. Have her checked by a veterinarian to determine if the problem is treatable, particularly if this is a recurrence.

Thyroid or other hormonal ailments may cause an abnormal season. Sometimes these can be treated and may keep the abnormality in abeyance until a breeding is accomplished. However, these as well as other infertility problems are often hereditary, and the question of whether to breed the bitch at all should be reconsidered.

Breeders have occasionally found that only every other season is fertile when a bitch cycles more than twice a year. In this case, proper planning is sufficient.

Muzzling

Prospective mates should always be introduced on leash. If the bitch—or, rarely, the male—is snappy or growly, don't take any chances: Use a muzzle. A leash, belt, adhesive tape, or even panty hose may be used in lieu of a muzzle. Loop the leash around the dog's muzzle twice, then cross behind the head and tie.

There is no sense chancing injury of the male if the bitch is resistant or in pain, or is just naturally a "bitch."

The mating may be poorly timed, or forced a day or two early or late. Some bitches, however, never agree to deflowering and, thus, a muzzle is a safety device. They are often more cooperative on the second breeding or after whelping a litter.

Prolapsed Prepuce

Prolapsed prepuce is a rare occurrence in which the sheath everts during erection. The penis is constricted so it cannot return to normal size. This was discovered to be the problem in a stud who, after a three-hour tie was finally broken, still maintained a painful erection. After cold-water immersion failed, he was taken to the vet. The condition can be manually or surgically corrected under anesthesia.

Artificial Insemination

Although it may not be as much fun for the dogs, AI is fairly simple. Although most AI's are performed by vets, many breeders are adept at the procedure. This is not for novices and should not be attempted without demonstration by a vet or other experienced person. Carelessness or improper procedure can cause injury to tender tissues.

The male must be stimulated, which is more easily accomplished by having an enticing bitch present. They're certainly more stimulating than you are!

The semen is collected in a receptacle, then deposited in the bitch by means of a pipette. Sterile equipment is a must, or an infection will result rather than a pregnancy.

This procedure is an aid when breeding aggressive partners or when a juvenile vagina, low libido, or obstructions present themselves. It is also the answer when the stud is injured, has arthritis, or is advanced in age. Some breeds are just not built to breed naturally anymore, and AI is commonplace.

If the reason for lack of interest or outside ties is a false heat, AI does not help. Undertaking artificial breeding should not be a last-minute effort, poorly timed. If a natural breeding is not proceeding successfully, take smears. If the procedure is properly handled and timed, conception success with AI is good. Depending on the reason for use of AI, insemination can be interspersed with attempts at normal matings.

Sealyham breeders note that show-conditioned males are often bred artificially, due to their short legs and heavy weight. A fifty to seventy-five percent success rate is reported with AI in a kennel of Sealys, Miniature Schnauzers and Scotties.

The stud will appreciate warm equipment, that is, at body temperature. Massage him to erection, then grip firmly just behind the swollen glans until ejaculation begins. Place the receptacle directly under the penis, until all three parts of the ejaculate are caught. At this time, the count and quality of sperm should be examined microscopically. It should have a milky tinge. The contents of the receptacle are transferred to a syringe.

Before inserting the pipette, investigate the vaginal tract with a sterile glove. Aim the pipette first upward, then, as the bony pelvis is reached, forward until it is near the cervix, which varies with the size of the bitch. *Don't force.* Be gentle and patient. When the pipette is in place, attach the filled syringe and depress the plunger. It is often helpful to inject some air after the semen to help propel it forward. Ties may be simulated by an artificial bulb or by feathering the vaginal walls (stroking with a finger). Keep the bitch's rear raised for about ten minutes—the equivalent of a tie. Crate the bitch and do not allow her to urinate.

Multiple Sires

Once you're pregnant, you're pregnant and you're safe . . . except with dogs, because they can be impregnated by more than one sire. A female should be kept away from other suitors throughout her entire season, whether a breeding is planned or not.

Even though the mid-cycle days are the best for conception, some bitches ovulate over several days. They continue ovulation even after conception, releasing many, many eggs. They may conceive a second or third time, days after the first fertilization has occurred.

It is conceivable (no pun intended) that a litter of five could have five different sires. Fertility differs in individual dogs as it does in humans, and one bitch may conceive easily and be fertile for several days. Another may release her ova at one time and be fertile only for hours.

Restrain your tempting lass from consorting with males during her season unless you are positive of her fertile days. Even then, you may stand helplessly by and watch toothless old Grandma mating with her great-grandson on the twenty-third day.

You may take your bitch to the stud, come home, and expose her to other males, assuming that's that. It's not so.

The American Kennel Club states that this is a no-no. "It is the position of the American Kennel Club that for a litter of dogs to be eligible for registration in the Stud Book of the AKC, the dam of the litter must not be mated with more than one sire during her season."

Mismating/Mesalliance

Sometimes the bitch makes her choice without consulting you. You may not know about that selection until it's too late. She surprises you by proudly presenting eight squirming squeaky All-Americans in the middle of the Persian carpet.

If, however, you observe the filthy beast put his paws on your Precious, you can do something about her poor choice of a mate. Don't bother with the bucket of water or the hose. Don't try anything else, either—any other method of forcing the delinquents apart is liable to cause damage to the dogs' reproductive organs and possible hemorrhage. Once the indiscretion is committed, you're too late to stop it.

It doesn't matter if the icy ducking does separate the lusty twosome: The deed is done. Then you're left with a sopping bitch, and most likely a pregnant one. Because you can be darned sure that the same bitch who misses every time you orchestrate an exquisite breeding, drive halfway across the country, and spend megabucks, will definitely take when the neighborhood Lothario does his thing.

Instead, see your veterinarian, who will administer a "mismate" estrogen shot. This must be done within two days to be effective, and preferably within twenty four hours. The injection prevents the ova from implanting in the uterus. The heat is extended. Normal litters may ensue.

If you had already made plans for a honeymoon, forget it. The ship is sunk for this cruise (see Multiple Sires, page 67). Contrary to those same old wives' tales of miscegenation, however, the elopement has absolutely no effect on subsequent litters.

Some breeders fear the mismating shot may cause conception difficulties during later breedings. This should be considered in a valuable producing animal. An alternative might be to allow the bitch to deliver the litter. If not purebred, the puppies can be placed in homes on spay/neuter contracts. Destroying the litter is an option some owners exercise.

Yet another solution open to the owner is to spay the bitch. The surgery is relatively safe in the first two weeks of pregnancy. It becomes more dangerous as pregnancy advances. If there are no plans to breed the bitch or show her in the conformation ring, this is a feasible choice.

One thing is certain—steps must be taken to control the urges. When a breeding is not desired by the owner, it will be by the concerned parties. If breeding is planned, the dogs may refuse the choice. There is nothing more frustrating than selecting a stud, then finding your bitch has settled on her own—the Heinz 57 variety next door.

6.   *IS SHE OR ISN'T SHE?*

There are impressive charts available to look up your pregnant bitch's due date. You find the date your girl was bred, and on the same line her due date appears. Actually, the easiest way is to count off nine weeks on the calendar.

Unfortunately, there are no tests that show whether or not a bitch is pregnant. An internal examination does not give evidence, either, and may actually introduce infection at a particularly vulnerable time.

If a bitch is carrying a large litter, she begins showing about the fifth week. The loin area puffs out, and is not concave when she is on her side. Breast enlargement begins at about that time as well. When the abdomen becomes greatly distended, many bitches exhibit discomfort, grunting as they lie down and changing position frequently. As their time nears, they cannot find a comfortable position. Most nest. Of course, by that time, you are certain.

If the litter is small or the bitch is large, well muscled or deep chested, evidence may not appear until the end of the nine weeks. The same is true of a bitch with a profuse coat, or of a maiden.

One woman wrote that her bitch did not look pregnant until the eighth week, but presented her with ten puppies. She isn't the only one who's been fooled. Many owners delight in picking due dates and number of pups. One family even has a lottery, or as they call it, a "littery." Experience has no advantage over the two-year-old's guess. People write of a bitch who looked as though she'd have six whelping twelve, another who appeared to be carrying three had eight, and yet another who at three weeks was *enormous* bore five.

Another fun method of guesstimation is suggested by Bulldog

breeders. Measure just behind the last rib on the last day of breeding. An increase in girth at forty days indicates pregnancy. Measure daily during the last week, counting one pup for each inch gained.

Milk does not appear until the last week of pregnancy, and occasionally not until after whelping. Movement of the pups cannot be detected until the last week to ten days. To feel movement, place a hand on the belly near the loin. Soon, watching the tiny kicks and swimming motions serves as an evening's entertainment. A slight pressure to this area may cause the pups to move. Which one will be the Champion? Will one be a guide dog or a Utility Dog?

But what about the bitch who keeps her hourglass figure, the one who is holding in her tummy just to drive her owner nuts? Some preparation is necessary, so subtle signs must be recognized.

With a maiden, the easiest sign to note is nipple enlargement. The nipples widen, even on a brood matron, sometimes to a half-inch or more at the base (next to the body). They often darken in color.

Appetite increases, even in the most picky eaters. However, that may also be true of those who only think they're pregnant. Some become droopy, sleeping an unusual amount, as though saving their strength for what is coming.

A personality change is another clue. A future mother who has enjoyed playing with other dogs may become cranky and grumpy, grumbling "Leave me alone" at others. Or, on the contrary, she often demands attention from her owners, as if to say, "You got me this way, now show me you love me, darn it!"

The vulva often stays slightly swollen, rather than shrinking up to its preseason state. In many cases, a string of crystal-clear mucus is seen. The backbone stands out near term, as it does on an extremely thin person. These are all considered good signs.

If you are still in doubt about the diagnosis, an X ray may be taken after the eighth week, when bones have calcified. At that time there is no damage to the fetuses from radiation.

Some expectant mothers leave no doubt as to their condition near term; they lie quite obscenely on their backs in all their rotund glory.

Palpating

Patience gives the same rewards as palpating, but most breeders are too antsy to wait for nature. This is especially true with long-planned litters, or titled dogs, or for those who have a bad track record in breedings.

Ideally, for palpation, you should have a small dog, a large litter, and long fingers. The dog should be relaxed and never obese. The optimum time to palpate for pregnancy is from twenty-five to thirty days. Later, it is difficult to feel anything because of the increased amount of amniotic fluid.

By grasping the entire belly in one hand, you can feel the uterus through the abdominal wall. As you move your hand from the rib cage toward the hips, the fluid-filled vesicles slip through your fingers, like a water balloon with knots tied at intervals. At this stage they are about the size of table-tennis balls.

This procedure takes a fine touch, and many veteran breeders (including the authors) find this a difficult task. By that time, your bitch is probably showing other signs anyway, and you will soon feel tiny kicks, rather than lumps.

False Pregnancy

Either you're pregnant or you're not. But your dog might fool you and herself. Dogs can suffer from a condition called "false pregnancy," medically termed pseudocyesis, which is caused by postestrus hormones.

The hopeful mother believes in every way she is in a maternal state. She may exhibit a distended tummy, enlarged nipples and breasts, and even milk. Some nest, pant, and have contractions.

If thwarted in their motherly instincts, some bitches adopt another small dog, kitten, or stuffed toy in lieu of their own pups. While this seems sweet to owners, the condition can be uncomfortable for the bitch. Severe cases bring cramps, caked breasts, and mastitis. Temperaments can change to downright crabby. They may show all or one of these symptoms.

The oddity is caused by a secretion of progesterone following estrus and ovulation. Although all bitches go through this period of increased hormone secretion, most do not show symptoms.

For those owners who have planned a breeding, it is a major disappointment when she—and they—tried so hard, all to no avail. The owner who has not bred his bitch is horrified to watch her blooming with the supposed evidence of her unbridled, albeit sneaky, passion. Do not scold the bitch. She can't help it. False pregnancy can develop whether or not she has been bred.

One hypothesis on the cause of this condition maintains that dominant females in the wild prevented others from mating and having pups. Not only that, the submissive bitch was sometimes forced to nurse the boss lady's kids. What alternative would a poor girl have but to imagine she was pregnant?

Indication of false pregnancy begins about six to ten weeks after the heat period (during normal "gestation" time), which is another reason owners assume the bitch is indeed pregnant. The episode usually ends within a couple of weeks.

No treatment is necessary for mild cases, though symptoms may be diminished by reducing food and liquids. Great discomfort may be treated with hormones. If the bitch's breasts are very full or uncomfortable, use hot packs, followed by cold packs, or pat with camphorated oil.

A normal litter may be conceived and whelped during the next cycle. Lowered fertility and smaller litters were noted in a Golden Retriever following a false pregnancy. Whelping a legitimate litter sometimes ends recurrences. If the condition is chronic, it is best to have the bitch spayed after the symptoms have subsided. During pseudocyesis, organs are enlarged, and there is danger of hemorrhage.

Morning Sickness

Some bitches suffer all the symptoms of their human counterparts. They are nauseous and refuse to eat during early pregnancy. Yellow bile is vomited from licking the mucous secretions.

Morning sickness is not harmful. Feed small meals of bland food, and call your veterinarian if it continues for more than a week or two.

At four weeks, the uterus enlarges to the point where it begins folding on itself. During that time appetite may wane, as a Sealyham breeder remarks. Continue her vitamins and keep coaxing with delicacies until she feels like eating again.

Touch Your Toes

An expectant mother can and should have normal exercise for the first weeks of her pregnancy. Strenuous exercise, such as jogging or high jumps, during this period is not a good idea, unless she is accustomed to it.

Continue her usual routine until her bulk becomes unwieldy. Most bitches know themselves when they should slow down. If yours doesn't curtail her own activity when her girth increases, you must. Continue moderate activity, such as walking.

Some bitches, on the other hand, will use any excuse to get out of exercising. In the words of a Bloodhound owner, "Inactivity leads to whelping problems. We jog our dogs (on a mechanical device) daily to ensure exercise, and have natural whelpers."

Feeding Expectant Mothers

Females are more fertile if a bit lean when bred. Obese bitches also have more trouble whelping. After breeding, they should be fed normally until the fifth week of pregnancy. Then you should offer them two meals a day, with additional protein, iron, and calcium foods

such as liver, hard-cooked eggs, and cottage cheese.
These not only supply the dam with sufficient nutrition for the pups, but aid in milk production. Too much liver causes diarrhea, so add small amounts. Raspberry-leaf tea added to the meal during gestation is touted by some people as an aid to free whelping.
Many breeders supplement the diet of the future dam with vitamins. The recipe that follows is an excellent natural source of protein and calcium.

Sooooooper Chicken

Save all your poultry skin, bones, and unwanted pieces. Place them in a crockpot and cover with water. (This is also a good way to make use of leftover broths and vegetables and their juices.) Sprinkle with garlic salt. Cook on high for five hours. Turn to low for another twenty hours. A pressure cooker decreases cooking time.

Scoop broth, bones, and all into a blender. Make sure bones are soft (large turkey bones must cook longer). Blend on high until completely liquid. Pour into empty containers and refrigerate or freeze, defrosting as needed. The mixture looks like chocolate pudding. Stir one heaping spoonful into regular meal.

The dogs don't have to be pregnant to enjoy this healthful concoction, and it costs little or nothing!

Resorption/Absorption

A bitch's breeding pattern has been normal; it is followed by actual signs of pregnancy, then suddenly . . . POOF! It's all gone, and you wonder if the pregnancy was wishful thinking. No wonder this phenomenon is pegged "phantom" pregnancy. In such cases the possibility of resorption should be researched and treated.
There is a school of thought that says all bitches conceive many fertilized eggs and resorb fetuses as a matter of course until the size of the litter is within her ability to carry and whelp. If something goes wrong, the process could continue until the entire litter is resorbed. There is no discharge or outward sign.
Resorption can be caused by injury, illness, medication, or hormonal problems. It usually occurs at mid-term, so an owner may not even realize the dog is pregnant.

A veterinarian should determine whether the bitch did conceive and what the cause of resorption may be. If the complication is diagnosed as low hormones, treatment with repositol progesterone, administered four weeks after breeding, may be recommended.

One Mastiff breeder administers an antibiotic during the third week of gestation to bitches that have demonstrated trouble with resorption.

Thought should be given to removing such bitches from breeding, as the condition may be hereditary. However, resorption does not happen as often as breeders believe. Most times there is a miss or false pregnancy.

Abortion

Canine miscarriages are rare. Infection, injury, malnutrition, or hormone imbalance may cause the loss.

The bitches' suffer little discomfort, as abortions occur before the fetuses reach full size. If there is evidence of bleeding or colored discharge from the vagina before term, see your veterinarian.

Take the bitch's temperature for about a week. An elevated temperature may indicate retention of fetuses or afterbirth.

Worms During Pregnancy

There are two theories concerning this dilemma. Of course, prevention is better than cure, but now and then a family of parasites moves in during the breeding interim or shortly thereafter.

Most breeders feel that if the prebreeding checkup was negative, the short time the parasites are harbored will not be injurious to the bitch or the pups. Deworming agents are toxic and breeders would rather not chance harming the whelps.

Others feel the pups develop better without the debilitating effect of worms. Use only veterinary-prescribed vermifuges and wait until after the first trimester.

The Labor Room

You've finally accomplished the breeding, and your gal is blooming with the blush of approaching motherhood. You may have despaired of reaching this point, but suddenly you realize D-Day is fast approaching, and you'd better have some place ready.

Choose an area that is away from the hubbub, but convenient and comfortable for you and the dam. Although some people select a corner of the kitchen or family room, most find it less than appetizing to have puppies, clean as they may be, performing their latrine duties as you bite into the lasagna. It's also more private for the mother and her brood to be away from the eye of the hurricane.

Many bitches still possess a den instinct, which telegrams, "Find a cubbyhole, get in, and nest like crazy." To forestall a poor choice on her part, select a place that pleases all of you. A spare room or corner of the basement or garage is a good choice. If she prefers a cozier environment, rig up an enclosure within her box—a removable partition—or a roof with hinges. Remember, you may have to join her in the box, and it should be possible for you to maneuver within the confines of her nest.

Once she starts the real business, she will likely forget about where she is. It is during her stewing and fretting beforehand that she eyes your waterbed or the soft carpet under the dining-room table.

The whelping box should be built, borrowed, or bought at least two weeks before due date. Paint the box with a lead-free paint, which can be disinfected and repainted between litters. There must be time to install her and convince her this is her new home. Feed her in it. Have her sleep in it. Pad it with cozy blankets and newspapers and let her mess it up to her pleasure.

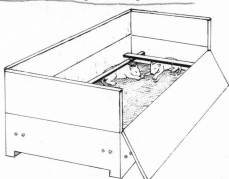

The box should be large enough for her and you during the birth, and for the mother to stretch at full length. It should be roomy enough for a large litter. Unless you plan to move the litter by three weeks of age—or less—it should also be high enough for older pups and sturdy enough for exuberant playtime. It is amazing how quickly the tiny, blind babes turn into rowdy, romping rascals.

The floor of the box should be raised on two-by-fours so that the litter will be protected from chill and dampness. Plywood makes a good floor. The plans that follow are for a box adequate for large breeds. The box may be scaled down according to the size of the breed.

The sides each have two pieces of lumber, one inch thick and nine inches wide. These are screwed to two one-and-a-half-inch bars. The box measures five by four feet. The front of the box has hinges between the two pieces of lumber so that it can be lowered for the dam to come and go with ease (though an anxious mother can scale astounding heights).

The top board at the front can be left down until the pups begin climbing. At that time, it can be raised and secured to the sides by hooks, so that all sides are eighteen inches high.

Inside the box, a rail should be placed three inches above the floor on all sides. The rail is about one inch thick and two and one-half inches wide, and is screwed to the sides from the outside. This serves as a guardrail for the pups, preventing them from being crushed against the sides by the mother. Dams are usually very careful about stepping around the pups and lying down, but with a large litter of helpless, fragile newborns, accidents can happen.

Now, sit back and wait.

7. *PACING THE FLOOR*

Breeders all endorse their own methods, systems, and superstitions, based on their experiences. All agree on one thing, however: Have a vet you can count on, one who knows you mean it when you holler "HELP!"

In the world of fantasy and commercials, the bitch has no amniotic stains or hanging teats. She is not panting in labor or chomping on a placenta. Nevertheless, she has just given birth to pups with open eyes and full coats that appear to be at least three weeks old.

In real life, things never go that smoothly. Keep the vet's phone number handy. Even the most seasoned breeders are more comfortable knowing the whereabouts of their vet, day or night, in case of an emergency. It's wise to have a veteran midwife on alert, as well.

Ten days ahead of ETA, the breeder should begin taking the bitch's temperature to chart her normal range. The evening temperature is usually higher than the morning's, so record both. Although gestation is normally from fifty-eight to sixty-five days, births do occur up to a week early. Large litters often arrive early, with small litters sometimes a day or two late. Ascertain the bitch's normal temperature pattern several days ahead of whelping.

The bitch that goes over the due date should be watched closely. Most breeders feel soothed by having the vet check the bitch daily when she is overdue. It seems like a chore, but it's well worth it if even one puppy is saved.

It is common for the bitch's temperature to be slightly lower than normal up to one week before whelping. In ninety-eight percent of cases a sharp decrease warns the big moment is due within twenty-four hours. At that point, it is advised never to leave the bitch alone. Whelping may start at any moment.

Stocky, short-bodied breeds are physically incapable of aiding themselves during the birth. So are bitches who carry such a large litter that their bulk prevents them from free whelping.

The owner should be present in case a bitch needs help or comfort. Sometimes the birth is too easy. The dam does not even realize a whelp is present and neglects to tear the sac. Occasionally, a bitch becomes hysterical and needs calming. It's been a long time since dogs whelped by themselves in the wild—and yours *never* has. Breeders report that most first-timers need tea and sympathy.

This is the time to put on a big pot of coffee, stack the clean towels and papers, and settle in for the wait. Your hands will be busy soon enough.

Whelping Kit

The basic whelping kit should include alcohol for disinfecting, plenty of newspapers for the actual whelping, a trash bag for soiled newspapers, your record book, heat lamp or other heat source, and non-skid flooring for the pups when all is done. Put in twice as many clean towels as you think you will need. You'll use them all. Place your trusty rectal thermometer and the petroleum jelly nearby.

Other equipment: a watch or clock to record births and labor time, hemostats or clamp, white thread, scissors, surgical gloves, and nasal aspirator. A baby scale is a nicety for large breeds and a necessity for Toys. A spare thermometer should be tucked in the kit, in case you become nervous and drop the first.

Some method is necessary for identifying all those squirming, identical little furry Sammy snowballs or golden Pekes-in-a-pod. Some people mark toenails with fingernail polish, but that wears off. A few clip a wedge of hair against the grain, but if you're on the wrong side you don't see it.

The majority of breeders use a neck tag ID. The best dog tag, by popular choice, is rickrack. It's available in a kaleidoscope of colors and widths (wide is best) and doesn't nestle into the fur, so it's not forgotten. Collars should be changed as needed. They can be checked daily during individual snuggle time and weigh-ins. As an economical plus, they can be washed and reused for future litters.

In a few weeks, those IDs serve for long-distance recognition while pups romp in the yard. When admiring buyers come to pick out their bundle of wagging tail and kissing tongue, you can tell them that Pink is a girl, Green is spoken for, Orange is smartest, Yellow is the smallest, and Purple is the best show prospect.

Among the requirements for whelping a litter are an extra large coffeepot and a good book. The polls show that running neck and neck for top contender in time-passers are name choices and first show plans for the as yet unborn pups. At this time, a friend makes good company and offers an extra pair of hands. If no friends are available, a spouse will do.

Ask old-timers in your breed about predisposition or breed-abnormality warnings (see Chapter 12). If you own Papillons, ask a fellow breeder or a Chihuahua enthusiast, not a Borzoi lover.

Groom the future mother. Trim long tresses away from the nipples and vulva. If you don't wish to cut away a glorious coat which took her two years to nurture and you to coif, leave the drape at the side and tie it back. Or use the method of one Lhaso Apso breeder—she dresses her gal in a body stocking, leaving the rear exit open and vents for the breasts.

Nesting *(tears & shreds)*

If you could believe your dog, one of the ecstasies of being an expectant mother is nesting. She tears and shreds with glee. You can almost see her smile. The blanket is an uncomfortable, lumpy bump in one corner, and the newspapers wouldn't soak up a tear in the

desert. You change papers and she starts anew, tossing them into the air, nesting with a passion.

This trait is a natural instinct and a common symptom. Some nest with a dogged scratch, scratch, scratch. Others wreak chaos with a vengeance.

Allow her to nest at will, though you should encourage her to do it in her box rather than in the petunia patch or your bed. German Wirehair Pointer owners learned this lesson quickly after a bedspread and two pillows were totally destroyed. Have fresh papers ready when the action kicks off. At the end, replace papers with good nonskid flooring.

Some bitches begin nesting halfway through their pregnancy, others wait until the last day, and a few never do. Each is normal in her own way.

A carry-over from the wild is the dam's bunny-soft undercoat, which loosens near the due date. The dam would pull out these tufts of fur to line her den as a cozy home for her infants. Nowadays, you should brush it out to avoid hair wafting about your house, your clothes, and the puppies' mouths.

Listlessness/Restlessness

As their time nears, many bitches alternate periods of deep sleep with flurries of activity. This means they are preparing for presentation of their babes.

One minute the bitch is sleeping so soundly she does not awaken to the usual temptations—food cooking, rattling of car keys, opening of the door. The next, she becomes restless, sensing that something is looming, though she's not sure what. She paces, crawls into minute cubbyholes, and follows you everywhere.

She wishes to escape from the household bustle and find a quiet place for privacy, yet two minutes later she returns to verify that you're still here should she need you. She wants your reassurance and loving touch.

As time passes, she becomes more urgent in her insistence, nesting and asking frequently to go out. Some bitches have accidents as pressure builds. She will be mortified if she goofs. Don't scold her, but you may find it easier on your nerves to install the bitch in her whelping box, letting her nest, tear, and pace to her content. A welltrained dog is an advantage, as the owner can put her on a "Down, stay." If you do not remain with her, check in every few minutes to assess progress.

Shivering

Just before whelping, some bitches quiver like a bikini babe in an Arctic storm. Though it might be through discomfort or fear of things to come, it is probably caused by her lowered body temperature. Reassure her if she is upset.

Most often, shaking ceases with the emergence of the first pup. She seems to realize, "Oh, *that's* what I'm here for."

If shivering continues throughout delivery, have the bitch examined following birth. One Welsh Corgi breeder relates that her bitch quivered throughout the whelping of eight healthy pups. The dam was uninterested in the litter. During the first week, four puppies died, fading within a day. She was treated with antibiotics for high E-coli count. After the first week, she resumed care of the pups. There were repeat performances in subsequent litters, resulting in the bitch being spayed. It is also possible to have this reaction from calcium deficiency (see Eclampsia, in Chapter 9).

Crying/Screaming

Some of us stub a toe and screech and curse. Others burst into tears, crying and sobbing. Or the reaction might be to moan bravely, or to tell everyone about the injury. And a few bear the throes of agony in silence and with clenched teeth.

The same is true of dogs. Of course, we don't have to listen to them cuss and tell us their troubles, but pain might be expressed aloud.

As the contractions escalate and the awareness of impending delivery heightens, some bitches cry and whimper their objection to pain and fear. A few breeds, Afghans for instance, are admitted screamers. Beardie and Miniature Schnauzer owners say their first-time mothers often yelp at the birth of the first pup. Breeders find that the first pup is often the largest, and the delivery seems easier after the first whelp has stretched and lubricated the birth canal.

Occasionally, a bitch shares her troubles with you for a couple of days in advance, making you as miserable as she is. This was evidenced by a Siberian Husky whose howls made her owners' nerves ragged in anticipation.

Panting

Women in childbirth-preparation classes are being taught to do what dogs have known all along: to pant. As delivery nears, panting accompanies other symptoms. Heavy panting may precede labor by as much as twenty-four hours.

The Green Light

Gestation is nine weeks, or fifty-eight to sixty-five days. There is as much as a two to four degree decline in the temperature of the majority of bitches, twelve to twenty-four hours prior to parturition. Sometimes they fool you—the temperature drops, then rises, then once again goes down, leaving you sitting home *two* days waiting for the event.

The temperature isn't all that drops. So does the belly. One morning you get up, and so does she, but her distended abdomen doesn't. She looks as though she could use a skateboard. This is particularly noticeable in the first litter.

Your bitch may refuse food a day before whelping. A few snack midway through delivery, but fasting is a good indication of imminence. The stringy vaginal discharge increases and thickens, and the vulva becomes soft and spongy, often much enlarged. Licking and hard panting escalate.

Labor

Reread this book, and then start reading a good mystery. Just about the time you get to whodunit, the bustle invariably starts. It's a sure cure for slow whelpers.

The bitch will try to find a comfortable position, and there are none left, it seems. She whines and shifts her weight. Many bitches peer comically at their rear quarters, as though trying to understand what this involuntary action of their bodies may be. Some panic, fearing that what they cannot stop is soiling the house. Talk to her with soothing words and caresses. Remain calm—at least outwardly—for the dam picks up the owners' tensions.

Examples of extraordinary rapport between breeder and dog are two cases in which the bitch halted her pacing to sit by her owner with a soulful expression in her eyes. The owners swear that when

asked, "Are you ready for your babies?" the bitch ran to her box and began the proceedings immediately.

In another case, a Yorkie was adamant about not starting labor until her owner sat beside her. Yet others, particularly kennel dogs, go to the other extreme, stopping all action until they have complete privacy.

You are soon able to see contractions. Your bitch strains and grunts as labor intensifies. She may move around and whip her tail (and amniotic fluids) against your nicely painted white box. She might crouch, as though passing a stool, or she might stand with a roached back. There is also the treasure who lies quietly on her side, calmly waiting.

Simple Whelping

The first visible sign of a pup is usually a bubble that appears at the vulva (as shown in the drawing that follows). Sometimes the pres-

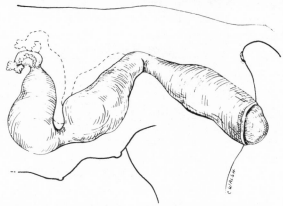

The placental bubble appearing at the vulva. Note other puppies still in uterine horn. Second uterine horn is indicated by dotted lines.

sure bursts the sac, lubricating the birth canal, helping to pass the first pup. Most times the puppy remains within its own membranes. Continual hard contractions should never last longer than fifteen to twenty minutes without being productive. Some bitches produce pups as easily as passing a stool; others must really strain.

An Irish Water Spaniel spews her pups out with centrifugal force. The midwife had better be prepared to catch the whelp, as must the breeder whose Bearded Collie delivers from a standing position. Ex-

perienced matrons frequently lie quietly or sit with hips to one side.

When the sac arrives intact, the bitch's first instinct should be to tear it open and lick the pup clean, rousing it to cry and move. If *she* does not, you must. Tear the membrane away from the head, and wipe the liquid from the mouth and nose. Vigorously rub the whelp as the dam would to encourage it to gasp and cry. There is no immediate worry about the cord. The first urgent necessity is to remove the sac and stimulate breathing.

The bitch shreds the umbilical cord with her teeth. If you must sever it, push the blood towards the pup. Tear the cord, about one inch from the pup, with a dull instrument or fingernails rather than making a clean cut. There will be less bleeding.

After the puppy emerges, the placenta may remain inside the dam. If she is quiet, there is no problem. It will pass before the next whelp. Some thrash about with the imminence of the next birth and could injure the attached pup. If so, clamp the cord twice and cut between the two. The hemostat next to the pup prevents bleeding, and the one next to the dam prevents the placenta from retracting.

Discourage the dam from continued tearing and chewing at the whelp's navel; this could cause damage or hemorrhage. If bleeding does continue, the cord should be tied with white thread, or a hemostat applied. A clamp used prior to cutting decreases bleeding. The cord should be severed on the placenta side—away from the whelp, with the hemostat between. Iodine may be used for disinfecting and cauterizing.

As a last attempt to stanch persistent bleeding, try this suggestion of a German Wirehair Pointer owner. Styptic® powder was applied, which not only stopped the bleeding immediately, but also dried the cord.

Bitches normally consume the placenta, then lick the pups clean and dry, stimulating the passage of the meconium (first stool).

Healthy pups cry and sniff for a nipple with heads raised and wobbling back and forth. The sucking reflex is surprisingly strong. One vet tells of a pup nursing on a back teat when only half out of the birth canal!

The classic head-first and rear-first positions are both common. If the emerging pup has the pads of its feet down, it will be born front first; pads up, rear first. A greenish discharge appears after each placenta, and a placenta with every pup. The dark reddish placenta may not appear until the next pup, but there should be one-on-one issuance. If the bitch does not object, move the pups to another box during each birth so they are not injured in the process.

"Dry" births, when membranes rupture before delivery, are also common. It is imperative to work quickly, so that the pup does not smother in the birth canal. At times, a pattern of one pup emerging soon after another, followed by a rest between those and the next pair, is seen. Release of a pup from each horn of the uterus is one theory to explain this.

Have water available throughout the labor, though few bitches will touch it. Some lap once or twice at broth in the middle of a large litter.

Dams commonly rest between puppies. Thirty minutes is the average length of R and R, but it may last up to as much as six hours or even longer. One Dalmatian bitch that whelps large litters sensibly takes rests of two hours between pups. Her breeder's records show she takes thirty-two hours to whelp eight pups. Don't act rashly or rush into hastening a normal delivery. The thing to watch for is straining. If there is none, there is no immediate alarm. However, most breeders would call their vet if the break lasts longer than three hours, to determine whether an oxytocin shot would help or if a cesarean section is indicated.

Breeders must learn to distinguish between mild and hard contractions. If intermittent hard labor continues for more than one and a half to two hours—or sooner if distress is apparent—a trip to the vet is demanded.

The new mother indicates the conclusion of the birth by relaxing and nurturing her pups. Her abdomen looks collapsed for the first time in several weeks.

Now—offer your proud dam a pick-me-up of beef broth, bouillon, or eggnog. We heard of some lucky Salukis who receive ice cream! After a rest period, take her out to relieve herself, wipe her up a bit with a damp towel, and clean up the messy box. You may have to force her, by leash, to leave her brood.

Adjust the heat lamp to the proper height. Move it to one side of the box if the dam is too warm. The pups seek out the warmth they need.

Indoor-outdoor carpeting is a popular choice for lining the box, as are fake lamb's-wool rugs. They're washable and easily replaceable. Do not use straw. It is prickly and irritating to pups' tender skin and can cause allergies.

The bitch should be taken to the vet within twenty-four hours of whelping for an exam and an oxytocin shot. Palpation or radiographs of deep-chested breeds and suspicious cases determines whether all is clear.

After a few deliveries, many breeders feel confident enough to administer the POP (purified oxytocic principal) when necessary during delivery. "When necessary" means *never* before the first puppy has dilated the cervix. Either the puppy *must* be born or at least a portion must be visible at the vulva. It is the practice of several breeders to give a POP shot (subcutaneously) midway through a large litter as a pick-me-up.

The dose is variable according to the breed size and brand of drug. Have your vet discuss usage of the product when you purchase the vial—ahead of time, please. Anybody who plans to breed more than once should learn how to give subcutaneous injections, for it is sometimes necessary to do so when a vet is not available.

For a time, a fad persisted in giving antibiotics to all dams after whelping. It is not necessary unless indicated (see Chapter 8). In fact, it may actually be deleterious to pups, causing diarrhea.

Write all statistics in your record book: sex, time of birth, color, markings, weight, and ID.

Remember: The most important requirement for a breeder—other than his dog—is common sense. You can do most anything if you have to. A teenager tells of whelping her first litter when her parents were gone. She woke up to find the bitch nesting under her cot in the whelping room, a week before due date. She flipped on the light switch and discovered the electricity was out, due to a thunderstorm raging outside. She managed to help a litter of seven come into the world by candlelight and kept the pups warm until the lights came on.

Consuming Placentas

Although some bitches turn up their noses at the placenta, most take to it as though it were a deluxe pizza. The slippery sac containing the pup is torn, the baby licked and cleaned. Then the dam turns to the task of eating the placenta. Others eat it first, chomping and slurping, before they tend to the pup. In those cases, *you* tear the sac. Occasionally, it may be consumed as the pup is delivered, with you never seeing it.

Consumption of the placenta, with its hormones, stimulates the milk flow, facilitates delivery of the following pup, and aids reduction of uterine size after delivery. Before domestication, bitches ate the evidence of a fresh birth to hide the litter from predators.

Opinions concerning placentas differ. Some breeders allow the bitch to consume all of them; others let the dam have two or three and dispose of the rest. A few people do not want the bitch to touch the placentas and prefer to handle the entire process themselves (in the trash bag, not in the manner of the dam).

The wisest course is to allow the bitch to follow her instinct. Do not get into a hassle over this issue, upsetting her. If the situation can be managed calmly, let her consume a few. Too many increase the discharge or result in diarrhea or indigestion. However, it is better to cope with diarrhea than a frantic bitch who has been thwarted in her efforts to do as nature is telling her.

Number of Pups

If you're mad at the male because you only had one pup, your anger is misdirected. It's the female that determines the number of pups— it depends on how many eggs are released during ovulation and how many are carried to delivery.

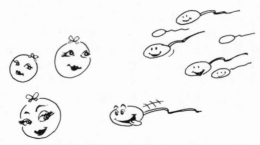

On the other hand, all those kings that divorced, or worse, beheaded, their wives for presenting them only with girls, were off base. It's the sperm that determines the sex. You know—those squiggly little things with the *X*'s that are the girls and *Y*'s the boys. Overall, the amount of males and females whelped pretty much evens out, although some males seem to produce a preponderance of males . . . or the reverse.

The important point to consider is not how many females or males you have, but how healthy and sound they are.

The Birds and the Bees

How do you tell a boy from a girl? In adult dogs, it's rather simple. *He's* the one who marks every tree, post, and fireplug as his territory. She's the one who presents you with the "Surprise!" nine weeks later.

With short-coated breeds, the reproductive organs and nipples are obvious. They aren't hidden by Calvin Klein jeans or Izod shirts.

Even a long-coated dog may be rolled over on its back for closer inspection.

Newborn puppies, however, are dogs of a different color. Even veteran breeders have been embarrassed at discovering that one of the "girls" wearing pink rickrack should have been wearing blue. It's best to double-check before forwarding the registration application.

Remember the childhood game of "Button, button, who's got the button?" Males and females both have buttons, but the location tells the story. The tinier the dog, the tinier the button, but it's always there. The male's is a minuscule penis, directly behind the umbilical cord. The tiny vulva is between the rear legs of the female, under the anus.

Though gender determination is not a priority at whelping, it is one of the first questions your friends ask. Even if the pups are not purebred or registered, gender is always of prime importance to the buyer. Everyone has a demand, and it's usually the opposite of the supply. Unfortunately, there are no surgical sex changes for dogs.

Even though their owners are sometimes confused, the dogs themselves never are, and that's what all the sniffing is about.

8. DILEMMAS AND DIFFICULTIES

It's when real whelping problems arise that you appreciate a professional working relationship with your vet(s). Don't sell yourself short; if you've bred for any length of time, you've probably seen a lot more normal whelpings than your veterinarian. But in the vein of professionalism, be ready with facts when you call for help.

Know the time the temperature dropped and the time the first contraction occurred. He'll need to know the interval between pups (if any have been born), the color of mucous membranes (gums), the current temperature, the pattern and current status of uterine contractions, the approximate number of pups left unborn (is she still huge?), the color of discharge, and the results of a careful vaginal exam.

Assessment by phone of all the data can allow you and your vet to decide if you're just worrying a bit early, if there's something *you* can do to help, or if the bitch needs immediate veterinary attention.

Vaginal Exam

Constant or unnecessary exams only serve to introduce trauma and infection. However, a vaginal exam may be necessary during an abnormal whelping. The exam is done with an index finger, or (in cases of large hands and/or small bitches) a little finger may suffice.

Scrub hands thoroughly and trim back nails—they hurt! You can use surgical gloves or do it barehanded, but in either case, a bit of petroleum jelly makes insertion smoother. Gently introduce your finger into the vulva and proceed slowly upward (toward the backbone). At the level just below the anus, the vagina becomes horizontal. Thus your path is first upward and then forward toward the head.

If the bitch were not in labor, you could not proceed this far. The tract would be narrow and tight and the bitch would vigorously resist the advances of your digit. During labor the vagina is dilated and although the bitch's head may still have to be held to keep her still, there is less resistance.

As your finger advances, you may either encounter nothing or bump into a puppy. Most commonly, you'll feel a head coming, nose first. Sometimes a live pup will begin sucking the end of your finger!

Once you've encountered a pup, by gentle probing, try to establish its position. Can you feel both feet next to the head? Is the forehead above or below the nose? Sometimes all you encounter are legs. Feet with pads up are hind feet, and pads down are front feet.

Now you are able to tell your vet the position.

Prenatal Loss of Fetuses

If there is a colored discharge prior to due date, let your vet know immediately. If this is too early for labor, an abortion is in progress. If close to term, a cesarean section or manual delivery of the dead pup may save the remaining litter.

A greenish-colored discharge or a foul odor before the first delivery suggest a dead pup. You must act quickly to save the others. If the birth does not commence, call your vet.

Primary Inertia

If the delivery date arrives but no puppies do, be alert for signs of primary inertia. The cervix is open, but no labor is in evidence. No puppies are born. If a water sac breaks, it might appear as though the bitch has wet herself. She does not always exhibit signs of distress. More than likely, she'll do nothing more than nest, pant, and wonder why you're so worried. Follow your instincts. This is when rapport between animal and owner is so important. Do not leave a bitch while labor is impending.

When there is a notable temperature drop (that stays down), labor should begin within twenty-four hours. If not, a cesarean is vital. This is an Emergency, with a capital *E*, and cannot wait until the morning. Waiting makes the difference between live and dead pups.

Primary inertia is fairly common in Toys, but can also occur in single-pup litters and bitches over five years of age in any breed. This condition can also be the result of obesity, hormonal deficiency, or lack of exercise. Overstretching, caused by uneven distribution or too large a litter, has also resulted in PI.

In one rare case of hydrops amnii, storage of too much amniotic fluid, a cesarean was necessary to salvage the pups. A bitch suffering from this malady is obvious. She enlarges soon after conception, her abdomen becoming immediately immense and unwieldy. The uterus is too overstretched for contractions to be efficient.

Of course, not every dog that goes over due date is a PI case. We know of a Min Pin who refused to do *anything* until the breeder was installed in the box with her. Then she settled down to business and free-whelped a normal litter. Another owner brought her bitch into the vet clinic each day when she went to work. Everything appeared normal, but the bitch had never gone over in prior litters, and she felt better having her watched.

Most bitches prefer having their owners present, as, for example, in the case of the vacationing owner, where the bitch held out three long days until the owner walked in the door.

Secondary Inertia

When the uterus tires and labor ceases or weakens, this is secondary inertia. When it occurs during a large litter or in an older bitch, the uterus may be fatigued or overstretched. This condition is common in many giant breeds, according to a Mastiff breeder.

Secondary inertia can also be caused by extremes—too long a labor, too large a fetus, too small a pelvis. Prolonged straining with a malpresentation or a dead puppy lodged in the birth canal can cause uterine exhaustion and cessation of labor.

Manual reduction of the impediment helps, but if contractions have ceased or weakened, they will have to be recommenced with oxytocin. This may intensify labor within ten minutes to help prevent loss of pups or the necessity for a cesarean. Remember proper usage of this drug. If it is given before the cervix is open, the uterus can rupture.

A Scottie breeder reports some success with a "lazy" bitch. With sterile gloves, she strokes (feathers) the inside of the vagina, which can have the same effect as POP. Some secondary inertias, even without physical blockage, will not respond to oxytocin. If, after a shot of POP and/or feathering, labor does not resume or is still unproductive, veterinary attention is required.

Size of Litters

Two or fewer puppies may not exert enough force for uterine contractions to begin. However, if you have charted temperature, you are aware of the time lapse before labor is expected.

The vet may be able to induce labor if the cervix is open, or to extract a puppy wedged in the birth canal. These cases must be aided by a vet or, if one is not available, by a veteran midwife. This is not a procedure for the novice breeder.

If a small litter is suspected, take X rays at seven to eight weeks. On the other hand, if the litter is large, primary or secondary inertia may occur. Oxytocin may help in these instances or a cesarean may be indicated.

Cesarean Section

You have read about some of the problems that necessitate a cesarean. Breeds with large heads and/or small pelvises are commonly sectioned. If your dog falls into these categories, talk to other breeders beforehand. Ideally, your vet clinic will have a high success rate on cesareans. One Bulldog breeder drives three hours to a vet who handles the surgeries by the method she has found to be most successful with her dogs.

While cesareans should not be routine, they are accomplished swiftly and are often lifesaving to both pups and dam. Many Toy, Sighthound, brachycephalic, and some other breeds, however, are hypersensitive to anesthesia.

For most surgeries, there are a wide variety of reliable anesthetics and your veterinarian uses the one in which he has confidence. Unfortunately, most commonly used anesthetics cross the placenta during a cesarean, resulting in very sleepy, weak, or even dead pups.

If your bitch is facing a cesarean, your veterinarian should be willing to discuss the choice of anesthetic. Familiarity with the drug and
safety for your bitch are desirable, but with a valuable purebred litter
the puppies' viability should receive equal consideration. After all,
the pups are why you bred her in the first place, aren't they?!

In cesarean sections where the bitch is still fresh and live puppies
are anticipated, the best choices are narcotics (morphine sulfate) or
narcotic/tranquilizer combinations (Innovar-Vet® from Pitman-
Moore) followed by a novocaine block along the incision line. This
creates a stage of relaxed sleepiness without pain in the mother and
does not make the puppies groggy.

A specific antidote to the narcotic agents (Nalline®, from the Merck
Company) can be given following surgery. But even without the antidote, breeders extol this method, saying their bitches are nearly
awake after surgery and can go home immediately. In one case, the
bitch actually walked out to the car, following her owner and the box
containing her squealing litter! They're often caring for their lively
brood in a few hours.

When a cesarean is scheduled, prepare a box to transport the pups
home. Line it with several layers of newspaper covered with a towel
or blanket, and bring an additional cover to keep the litter warm.

After a cesarean, the pups could be a little sluggish for a time, and
the new mother may seem uninterested in them. Natural birth process stimulates the hormones and the maternal instincts, especially
in first-litter bitches.

Introduce the pups to the mother cautiously and with constant supervision. You might have to wait until she's completely awake.
Heed the warning of a breeder who lost two pups when the dam
groggily snapped at and killed them. Unfortunately, at this time, she
cannot tell the difference between her babes and an enticing pork
chop.

Reassure the dam. Keep the pups warm and cozy until Mom is
awake. Offer a nipple to one pup at a time, and soon she will respond.

Encourage the puppies to nurse the colostrum. Hold them to the
nipple and extract the first milk into each one's mouth. Usually this
is enough to stimulate interest. Otherwise, wait a few hours and attempt again.

Depending on the reason for the surgery, bitches may deliver subsequent litters naturally. If surgery is needed a second time, serious
thought should be given to the question of further breedings. If the
cause is too narrow a pelvis or primary inertia, your bitch's daugh-
ters could be inheriting the same tendencies. The exception would

be certain breeds (see Appendix, Breed Predispositions) where the planned cesarean is the norm.

Discourage extreme activity, such as jumping. Examine the dam's incision daily for signs of infection. The stitches are removed after ten days. As with all animals after surgery and postpartum, a temperature should be taken daily. The normal postpartum temperature is one degree higher (102.5°–103°F, 39.1°–39.4°C) with a section.

Malpresentation

These are some abnormal birth positions that may require assistance: head with only one front foot or neither; only one rear foot; or tail only (butt first—true breech). In these cases, attempt to snare one of the legs that is caught and pull it into the correct position.

Sometimes gentle retraction, pushing it back from whence it came, allows the offending part to come into place. If you feel that a pup is upside down (forehead below nose, or nose with foot, pads up), you can attempt rotation if any part can be grasped.

One or both front feet showing (pads down) with no head adjacent is an indication of a "wry-neck" pup (as shown in the drawing that follows). The head is turned back and the bitch is attempting to deliver both body and head side by side. These pups are usually impossible to deliver, and the pup is dead from asphyxiation. A sideways presentation of back or belly is likewise unrectifiable.

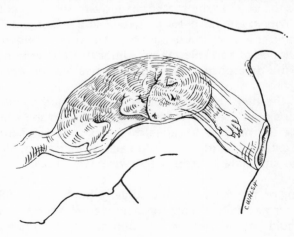

Wry-neck presentation

A malpresentation that is not remedied in one or two attempts is a signal for vet attention and possible cesarean. *Do not* pull on a pup until it is in a normal delivery position.

Getting a Grip on Things—Assisted Delivery

If the pup is in normal position but is just stuck, assisted delivery can be lifesaving. This is common with the first pup in the litter.

Extracting a pup is not for the meek and mild. People are terrified of pulling off a leg or a tail. This is extremely unlikely unless the pup is already dead and partially decomposed. (Pups are sturdier than you think.) Allowing the pup to remain wedged in the birth canal not only causes the death of that pup but may also cause the death of the others and extends the pain of the bitch.

If legs are protruding, time is of the essence. If the pup does survive, there may be other consequences. Lack of circulation during delivery can lead to gangrene, which in one case resulted in the loss of a pup's ears and half a foot at one week of age.

Stand the bitch or lift her abdomen, taking advantage of gravity. This is where two people come in handy. Give POP if contractions have ceased. Use a rough cloth or towel—pups are slippery. Pull toward her hocks *with* contractions. Exert pressure firmly and evenly towards the dam's hocks. Rotate the pup. Do not jerk.

Enormous Pups

Extremely large puppies may lodge in the vagina—assuming they can pass even that far. It is frustrating and urgent when a pup is wedged and birth is delayed.

Sometimes a little elbow grease—combined with petroleum jelly—is all that is needed (see previous section, Getting a Grip on Things). At the same time, you may need a third hand to hold the bitch or to aid in the birth. Peel the tight vulva around the pup, allowing more of it to slip out of the vagina. Exert pressure on the perineum (the area between the anus and vulva).

This is painful, and even the most docile bitch might snap at the hand that is helping her. A very understanding partner to aid you at this time is helpful. Non-doggy people may not feel the life of the pup is worth the pain of a bite. Act quickly, and everyone's agony will be over shortly.

If all else fails, the bitch should be taken to the veterinarian for an episiotomy. This vulvar incision should not be a routine procedure as it must be stitched and will be sensitive. However, there may be no alternative.

If you are unsuccessful in dislodging the whelp, it will be lost, and a cesarean may be necessary to save the rest of the litter. The wedged pup may be dead before you can get to the vet. You cannot wait; you must act at once.

Prolapsed Vagina

Although prolapse can occur in any dog, it is most common in the Mastiff-type breeds, which are prone to vaginal hyperplasia. Just prior to or during whelping, part of the vagina everts, presenting a rather gruesome red ball of tissue at the vaginal opening. Although this is easily replaceable by your vet, swelling may not recede enough to allow vaginal delivery of the current litter, thereby necessitating a cesarean. In at least one case of vaginal prolapse that we know of, the bitch whelped normally thereafter.

Vaginal hyperplasia in another bitch was corrected with surgery. Cesareans were necessary after the surgery, due to postsurgical adhesions.

Prolapsed Uterus

This is a very rare condition in which prolonged straining continues after all pups have been delivered, perhaps because of a retained placenta. If this is allowed to go on, the weakened organ can turn inside out.

A long, rather gory mass extends from the vagina, often to the hocks. It may be Y-shaped if both uterine horns are involved. Wrap the organ in a clean, damp cloth and get to the vet, who will reinsert the tissue where it belongs (anesthesia will be used). Immediate or subsequent spaying might be recommended.

Uterine Torsion

Torsion results when one or both horns of the uterus twist. The path to delivery is shut off, as are the blood vessels of the uterus. The bitch labors without delivery, or never begins. Labor may start and stop, and the bitch could appear depressed and in discomfort, often with abnormal crying or moaning. The gums may be a dark, muddy red, or white with shock. If in doubt, compare the gums to other dogs' mouths. The bitch may have a mental vagueness or even become comatose.

If the breeder is unaware of the situation, infection from decayed fetuses usually requires spaying or may even prove fatal. Pups and dam will die unless the breeder is alert to the trouble and acts swiftly, seeking veterinary help.

Complete uterine torsion in a German Shepherd bitch was noted in our survey. When the bitch braked in mid-labor, the novice breeders listened to poor advice and waited three days for delivery to resume. The end result was dead pups, causing a ruptured uterus, peritonitis, and eventual death of the bitch.

Partial uterine torsion can also occur. One breeder lamented keeping watch and consulting with her vet on an overdue bitch. When no labor had begun on the sixty-eighth day, she insisted on a cesarean. The partial torsion had lowered blood supply for the last two weeks of gestation, retarding development of the fetuses and resulting in the belated birth. The "pseudo-preemies" weighed seven to thirteen ounces less than normal.

Ruptured Uterus

A rupture can be the result of an overanxious, misguided breeder who administers oxytocin before the cervix is open. Abdominal injury can also cause traumatic rupture of the uterus. Infection or prolonged contractions—usually with dead pups, or putrefying afterbirths—causes tissue death in the uterine lining, leading to rupture. Ruptured uterus has also been recorded as a sequel to vaginal hyperplasia surgery.

Symptoms are shock, pale mucous membranes, a rigid abdomen, and/or an extremely high temperature, up to 106 degrees.

The only chance for survival is to speed to the vet. Fortunately, uterine torsion, prolapsed uterus, and ruptured uterus are extremely rare.

Mummies

Mummified fetuses are startling and horrifying. Mummies are dead and dehydrated fetuses retained within the uterus. They are undersized and withered, and are often delivered along with normal live pups.

A breeder of large dogs said, "I knew it was tiny (three ounces). In breaking open the sac, the skin started to peel off the fetus. The rest of the litter produced another mummy, three pups that expired during the birth, and five normal pups." In the following litter, the cervix did not dilate, and a cesarean produced one mummy and one live pup. Spaying was recommended in that case. However, an occasional mummy in an otherwise normal litter is no reason for concern.

Twins

Two pups trying to emerge at once will lodge in the birth canal or at the vulva. You must make a difficult choice: Push one back, and allow passage of the other—preferably the stronger one, since the other will be without oxygen and may die. Delivering one pup usually allows birth of the second without difficulty and in short order.

Lifeguard Techniques

When pups remain in the birth canal too long or inhale fluid, revival techniques may turn the situation from disaster to celebration. Revival methods will also aid surgically delivered pups to become alert.

Various methods are used by breeders to stir vitality: removing secretion from the mouth and nose, artificial respiration, rubbing vigorously, oral solutions, and the "shake-down" or "swing" method. To shake down a pup, cushion the puppy's neck and back in your hands with its head down. Swing the pup in a wide downward arch. This dislodges fluids and encourages circulation.

Insert a finger into the pup's mouth. Gagging can rouse the breathing reflex. While giving mouth-to-mouth resuscitation, gently squeeze the rib cage.

Enthusiastically recommended by one German Shorthair Pointer breeder is Dopram®, a respiratory stimulant. She states she would not be without it during a delivery. One drop on the tongue of "blue" pups (pups suffering from lack of oxygen) gets them going. Your vet will probably use it in a similar way on cesarean-delivered pups. However, for those who are without it, use a drop of brandy or make a glucose solution—a tablespoon of honey or corn syrup plus a dash of salt to one cup of boiled water. These solutions should be administered a couple of drops at a time from the fingertip or by eyedropper.

An ingenious breeder of Irish Water Spaniels taped a failing puppy to a bread board, which left her free to tend the rest of the litter. She put a heating pad on the board, taped the pup's hind feet, and slanted the board at a forty-five-degree angle, with the pup's head hanging down. She said, "I sort of batted him around a bit until he squirmed. When he stopped, I would nudge him some more. I really annoyed that pup for about a half hour. His nose ran and I wiped. He squawked a bit too. I didn't think he had any fight in him but he must have. It cleared his lungs. After that I gave him some honey and boiled water and put him back, feeling I had done all I could. In a day I couldn't tell which pup it was!"

When pups are chilled, or when they are under the average weight, warm them before giving any food or stimulant. A chilled pup cannot digest food, and it may kill him. A hint for warming puppies is to get them close to the breeder's skin, in an inner pocket, a T-shirt, or even a bra! Another way of warming them is by holding them in lukewarm water.

How much is too much? Although most of us hesitate to give up, when the struggle continues for more than a couple of days, pups often have to be put down later. One breeder tells of extreme methods used to keep puppies alive in three instances: one was still at birth weight at four weeks, the second was diagnosed as having a bone deformity at ten weeks, and the third was discovered to be suffering from patent ductus at eleven weeks. All were euthanized.

Yet another breeder tells of a puppy who survived, thrived, and attained his Championship! Of course, obvious birth defects, as described in Chapter 10, should be checked.

Premature

Breeders' accounts show puppies growing to normal adulthood who are born up to one week in advance of their due date. Premature puppies from a later breeding, given the misnomer "runts," can be whelped as part of a term litter.

Breeders tell a variety of unusual stories. During a much anticipated and last-chance breeding, four matings were accomplished. The first two were reluctant and so were backed by the second two, with an eight-day breeding span. The dam got extremely large, and on the due date from the second breeding, a tiny pup missing some hair just "popped out" with no contractions or other signs, according to the breeder. The remaining seven pups were born two days later. Two of those were also missing hair. Although the first puppy died, the rest of the litter survived.

In another case, a preemie Samoyed survived but was behind in pigmentation and coat development for several months. If the puppies are normal but small, supplemental feeding and warmth should save them. Eventually, they will catch up.

Be Prepared

Although we would wish for the sake of all females and their owners that you never need this chapter, the likelihood is that if you continue breeding, you will. If the owner is prepared, realizes what is happening, has this handbook nearby, and knows when to call the vet, then this chapter has served its purpose.

9. FOR WOMEN ONLY

Take good care of the dam. Daily, you see evidence of what she has done for you.

Check her temperature twice a day. Temperature is commonly elevated one degree the first day or two. Trouble is usually first preceded by an elevated temperature (103°F or higher, 39.4°C or higher), possibly signifying infection of the uterus or mammary glands. Your vet should be consulted quickly, so that the appropriate antibiotics and other therapy can be initiated. Aspirin helps lower fever. Offer plenty of liquids.

Postwhelping discharge is greenish black or dark red immediately following delivery. This sometimes lasts for a day or two, then turns to a brownish red for one to three weeks. If it lasts longer, contains fresh blood or pus, or is discolored, bring the dam to your vet.

Carrying the newborns around for the first week or two is not uncommon behavior, especially for those dams who usually seek the smallest nook in the room. This tends to make owners nervous. It is also possible, of course, for the pups to be injured. See if you can quiet her, calmly. She may cease the pacing if you can make her den cozier—cover it with a blanket, make it smaller or darker, or eliminate traffic and noise in her room.

Lack of Maternal Interest

A spoiled bitch that thinks of herself as a person rather than a dog might not behave maternally. This female begrudges being shut away from the family. All these yammering noisy little creatures are bringing her pain and trouble . . . and jail.

Her people are insisting she do all types of disgusting things, such as bathing puppies (with her tongue, yet), feeding puppies (when she's so doggoned hungry herself), and worse yet, "pottying" them. She didn't ask for this, they did. But she's the one doing the work. Well, she'll just show them—she won't.

So the owner has to break the sacs, clean the pups, put them on the nipple, hold Mama still while the babies eat, and take over latrine duties. It's time-consuming, and owners wonder why on earth they planned this. The mother acts totally bored, and the minute her human family leaves the room, so does she. A dam with this attitude should be watched for animosity toward the pups.

An immature dam may behave this way with her first litter and improve with her second. Sometimes just a few days suffice, until the new mother discovers she's a dog. There are exceptions who are genetically lacking in maternal instincts.

Warnings abound in our survey that spoiled household pets are the worst mothers and exhibit lack of interest. Kennel dogs seem to be more instinctive. To avoid this problem, treat the dog like a dog, not like a human.

Some dams feel if they don't look at their pups, they will go away. Unfortunately, they might. If the dam won't care for them, the owner must or the pups will die.

The lack of interest, however, might signal infection. Watch for abnormal discharge. Take out your trusty thermometer and use it.

A dam who has experienced a cesarean, particularly a first-time mother, may not show interest in her litter. Encourage her interest by rubbing her milk and scent on the puppies. Be patient. If she is not ready to yield to motherhood, wait a bit. The colostrum can be utilized for up to twenty-four hours postpartum. The immediate vital need is warmth.

If a dam appears hostile, do not force her to stay with the pups except during feeding. Stay with her, seeing that she does not harm them. Breeders of Rottweilers cautioned that some literally must be muzzled to allow pups to nurse. Hostility is not isolated to this breed, but can be true of others as well.

If the room is kept warm and the pups are gaining weight, the dam does not need to be with them constantly. Socialization can be provided by you. Tranquilization of a nervous mother may help.

If only one puppy is rejected, the breeder must warm and feed the pup if it is to survive. The rejection might be due to the pup's undetected illness or defectiveness; it is a dormant survival-of-the-fittest instinct.

Feeding the Crew

The mother should be given anything that turns her on—and lots of it. The usual fare—decked out with broths, cottage cheese, and liver—is appealing. She should be eating at least twice as much as she normally does, and more if she wants it. For the first day or two, feed her wet and sloppy food, encouraging her to chow down.

Use whatever tricks you need to entice her. Warm the food, sprinkle it with garlic salt, cook a stew, feed her your leftover goodies, use gravies: anything that works. This is the one time you should cater to her tastes in whatever way is necessary. Her caloric need while nursing is immense. Without TLC, she—and her dependents—will deteriorate.

Losses

Though not common, it remains a sad fact that losses do occur. If owners absolutely cannot face the possibility of loss of puppies or the dam, they should not breed.

Dams are sometimes lost through trauma or infection, leaving the pups orphans. Fathers are no help in this instance. A breeder cannot become hysterical at losses. Otherwise, what is sad and disappointing may be turned into a tragedy by further loss.

If the litter is lost, special care for the mother will include soaking the breasts with cool, wet towels to help dry up milk. Cut back on food and water. Lactation dries up in one week. Do *not* strip out milk: This stimulates production of more milk. The owner must be alert to caked breasts or other signs of mastitis.

Emotional support will also be necessary for the grieving mother. Some dams seem to be able to count and know if even one pup is missing.

Orphans

Loss of the mother means that the puppies must be fed by bottle or tube. They must also be massaged to stimulate urination and movement of the bowels. Orphan puppies should be handled and caressed frequently. You'll need to keep them clean, warm, and dry.

Anyone who is too fastidious to help their puppies will soon have no puppies to help. Pups cannot relieve themselves unaided until about two weeks of age. Soak a cotton ball or washcloth in warm water or baby oil and rub the genitals until the urine flows, and the anus until the stool is passed. This should be done each time the pups are fed. Most puppies have about two or three stools a day.

During the grooming session, use a clean, moist cloth to wipe the eyes. The dam bathes her puppies' faces each day, aiding eyes to open.

Rig up an incubator, using a box, a heating pad, and a towel. Exposure of the pups to any potential contamination should be avoided, particularly if the colostrum was not received.

If the sucking instinct is unsatisfied, pups sometimes suck on littermates. A pacifier coated with a yummy substance, such as sugar water or formula, might help allay the desire. If not, they should be separated. Once the teeth come through, damage can be caused to the others. In one litter, sucking resulted in injury to an ear and to a penis.

You can try the routine of feeding every two hours, or feed when the puppies cry. The latter way is particularly appealing at night. Puppies sleep through most of the night by the age of one week.

Hold the pup in its natural nursing position, belly down and head raised to nipple; otherwise, milk can be inhaled into the lungs. After bottle-feeding especially, hold the pup on your lap and rub its back until it burps.

Bottle-feeding is difficult, if not impossible, with large litters. Assistance must be solicited, or the results will be as frustrating as feeding quintuplets: One session is barely finished, and it's time to start again (see Hand-Feeding, in Chapter 10).

Commercial substitutes for dam's milk are good, but can be prohibitively expensive. Instead, use one of the following recipes, warmed to body temperature.

Almost like mom's

1 can evaporated milk (15 oz)
2 egg yolks
1 carton plain yogurt (8 oz)

For bottle feeding, add 6 oz boiled water

Supplement or supper

1 can evaporated milk
2 cans water

2 packages unflavored gelatin (dissolve in cold water, heat and
   blend)
2 beaten egg yolks
1 tablespoon cream (or Half-and-Half)
1 tablespoon honey (reduce if stools become loose)

Mix together

Both mixtures can be mixed in a blender, stored in the refrigerator,
and heated to body temperature for feeding. Commercially available
goat's milk is also an excellent substitute for mother's milk.

Foster Mothers

In the event that the puppies are orphaned or that the mother is un-
willing or unable to feed them, a foster mother may be an alternative
to bottle- or tube-feeding. Choose a dam that has a small litter, has
just weaned her own pups, or has lost her litter.

Bitches with a great maternal instinct may welcome the adopted
pups. Not all will be eager, however. Let the foster mother's milk
accumulate until she is uncomfortable, then rub the pups with her
scent or with milk.

Introduce the pups to the foster mother with care. The breeder
should watch closely to see that rejection or injury does not occur. If
there is any animosity, switch to hand-feeding (see Chapter 10).

If no foster mother is available, a retired matron can assist with the
cleanup chores. In at least one instance, the sire, a German Shepherd, took over everything except nursing!

Infanticide

Whether it is accidental, an overreaction to fear, or comes from a distorted sense of protection, infanticide is still shocking to the breeder. Prevention is just one more reason someone should be present during whelping. During consumption of the placenta or chewing of the cord, the whelp may be accidentally injured or even killed.

Care should be taken to assure that the dam has privacy and is not uneasy about her new family. If she is upset in any way, discover the cause. At the least, a jittery mother will incite her pups to be skittish, and at worst, she may injure or kill the pups in her nervousness.

Some bitches become overprotective and do not want anyone but their human family around their babies. Some don't even want their own people handling the pups. If this is the case, humor the new mother. Do any necessary handling while the dam is out relieving herself. Keep the peace.

Other dogs around the mother's territory are intruders. Even the best of friends occasionally become enemies when another dog, particularly another female, becomes curious or challenges the new mother for dominance. In one instance, a fight resulted in a laceration on the dam's breast, forcing a mastectomy.

Another unhappy ending followed when kennelmates burst into the nursery. A litter was destroyed. The owners were unsure of which dog killed the pups, but it made no difference. The dam had carried one pup outside and sat on it, perhaps for protection. This bitch remained fearful of the whelping box with subsequent litters.

If the dam wishes to leave the pups and be with her people, allow her freedom. Spoiled pooches do not understand the seeming imprisonment of being shut away from their human family. Puppy losses are sometimes attributed to lying or stepping on a pup. This happens more often in large litters.

Infanticide may be provoked by a physical cause: The dam should be checked by a veterinarian to eliminate any uterine or breast infection, high temperature or other problem. A reported incident of infanticide showed the dam to have a raging 106.5° fever. Do keep a temperature chart. Antibiotics control even a low-grade infection. When the dam feels better, she behaves better.

An unruffled owner helps the situation. A neurotic owner makes a neurotic pet.

Should the dam truly be uninterested in her pups or even antagonistic, steps must be taken to avoid injury to them. Muzzle the dam or take her away from the litter. If the dam is antagonistic, a foster mother may be introduced, but she often needs as much supervision as the reluctant dam.

The nursery period doesn't last long. If necessary, the pups can be weaned as early as two weeks if the mother is still acting abnormally. After so many months of planning, any awkward situation can be tolerated for two weeks.

Eclampsia (Milk Fever)

Though occasionally developing before delivery or up to six weeks postpartum, eclampsia appears most often during the first three weeks. It is caused by a deficiency in serum calcium due to a malfunction of calcium metabolism. Small dogs, especially Toys, are cursed with this problem.

Symptoms are rapid breathing, restlessness, nervousness, and whining. A victim staggers or has stiff limbs. Breeders report other weird behavior, such as bitches attempting to climb walls, hide under furniture, or maul or even kill pups.

There can be a pinched look around the face, exposing the teeth. Muscle twitches may be seen or felt. The bitch will shiver and be glassy-eyed.

If not treated, eclampsia eventually leads to convulsions and death. Since the immediate loss of calcium is through the milk, early mild symptoms might be controlled by removal of the pups.

Severe symptoms constitute an emergency and must be attended by the vet, not the breeder. A calcium solution is administered intravenously or subcutaneously. Careful medical supervision of these treatments is important as an overdose or too rapid administration can cause heart stoppage.

The difficulty is usually caused by a body deficiency, complicated by the increased draining of calcium supply by the pups. It is untreatable by adding calcium to the diet, and high calcium fed during pregnancy may actually increase risk. This condition often recurs with each litter. Bitches who have a history of eclampsia may routinely be given calcium injections prior to and following whelping. Pups must be removed and hand-fed.

Mastitis

Mastitis can occur in mothers who have weak, small litters or in a mother whose pups have died, leaving her with some breasts engorged. One bitch with inverted nipples had only two breasts from which pups were able to nurse. The remaining breasts had to be milked to avoid mastitis. Mastitis can also occur if mothers have an overabundance of milk, or if puppies scratch breasts, causing infection.

Inflammations are red, hot, and painful. The breast may appear bruised and be hard or caked. Mammary glands should remain soft, though full. Compare one to another to check. The dam often has a high fever, refuses to eat, and is depressed or restless. She may vigorously resent the pups nursing.

Milk from affected glands may be blood-tinged, discolored, and yellow or stringy with pus. Healthy milk appears like that bought in the store. Use a glass to test the color and texture. "Bad" milk clots on the glass.

Do not allow pups to nurse from an affected breast. Either wean the pups or cover the infected "faucets." Antibiotics are necessary to treat the dam. Warm packs help; aspirin eases the pain. If untreated, the skin will peel away from the affected areas, and the breast may be permanently lost.

Mastitis also appears during false pregnancy, usually in the two heavy rear breasts. Infection can follow bruising. Prevent a heavily uddered bitch from running and jumping—these activities invite injury.

Pups should also be dosed with antibiotics if they show signs of discomfort from ingesting infected milk. If the decision is to wean the pups, reduce the food and liquid intake of the mother.

To help prevent mastitis, see that pups nurse from all breasts, or milk the breasts yourself twice a day.

Acute Metritis

An abnormal discharge after whelping, accompanied by a fever, indicates a possible uterine infection. Rather than a slight reddish tinge, the discharge can appear to have the consistency and color of tomato soup. A foul odor is often present.

In severe cases, the bitch becomes toxic with lack of appetite and depression. She may vomit, be thirsty, and have diarrhea. The mucous membranes have a brick-red, muddy appearance. Temperature above 103 degrees is dangerous. Whether caused by retained fetuses or placentas, or by infection acquired during whelping, medical attention is essential.

The bitch is treated with antibiotics and other therapy. The pups should be watched for adverse reaction. Check the milk. Mastitis is often a sequel to metritis.

Puppies that have acquired the infection will cry from cramps and have diarrhea. They, too, must be dosed with antibiotics and hand-fed. Give lactobacillus to the pups.

In some cases, hospitalization of the dam may be necessary. If un-treated, metritis leads to spaying or to death (see Pyometra, in Chapter 3).

10.   *The Nursery*

At last, at last, you breathe a sigh and figure the worst is behind you. The pups have been safely born, and now you can just sit back and let the mother do the work. Let's hope you're right.

As you're watching these little bundles of hope squirming around the whelping box, you notice they move almost constantly. Blindly, they follow their noses to the source of their warmth and full tummies. Even when sleeping a front leg jerks, then the head moves, with a kick of the rear leg. Pups also demonstrate a homing instinct, better than that of the best pigeon's.

They squeak now and then, and show the power of their lungs when mama bumps them, or when they're stuck on the other side of her, or when you pick them up. But overall, the sounds are murmurs of contentment, similar to the sounds of a swarm of bees.

The puppy in danger is listless and shows little interest in nursing. The body is limp when you pick it up and the pup does not protest, nor does it nuzzle in a vain attempt to find a food source. The cry is either a weak and pitiful sound or a constant wail. Or, a sick puppy may be hyperactive, frantically moving about, often away from the others.

You should note the consistency of stools and whether the anus appears red and angry. Cleanliness is highly important. Contamination by the stool of even small scratches may lead to gangrene.

Even at this tender age, you cannot escape certain chores. You must cut the nails weekly, trimming off the tiny hook on the end of each one. Don't forget the dewclaw! The sharp nails can injure the dam's breasts and the extremely vulnerable eyes of their littermates and bring infection to both. Minor scratches on the dam's breasts can be soothed with petroleum jelly.

Acclimate the pups to noise. We live in a noisy world, and seldom do our dogs live in deserted areas where there is nothing but an occasional breeze. We live with slamming doors, dropped pots, children's noises, other animals, cars, video games, and vacuum cleaners. Therefore, they will also live with noise, unless you're selling them to hermit shepherds. Even then you'd better practice mooing or baaing.

Newborns

"Activated sleep" is normal in newborns. It develops the muscles, since at this stage, ninety percent of the pups' time is spent sleeping. In fact, when a puppy is ill, the first sign is listlessness and cessation of the active sleep. The breeder's dreams are fulfilled by watching the puppies "chasing bunnies."

Not surprisingly, the other ten percent of the pups' time is spent eating. Healthy pups squirm eagerly to the breast, latching tightly onto a nipple. When nursing and satisfied, their back legs and tails stretch straight back.

Many Toy breeders administer a drop of glucose solution at birth (see formula under Lifeguard Techniques, in Chapter 8). If necessary, this mixture can be used every hour or two to increase energy. If the puppy has not perked up by that time, see your vet.

The normal puppy temperature is 94°–97°F (36.1°C) during the first week. If a pup becomes chilled, warm it first before offering food. A temperature below 94° means serious trouble.

The most urgent requirement for the pups during these first few days is warmth. As soon as they are born, towel them dry. Keep their area warm and cozy. Pups will warn you by crying and panting if they are overheated. Remember, during the first two weeks, their temperature reflects that of the environment.

Eyes open in ten to sixteen days. Ears begin their duty at thirteen to seventeen days. The needle-sharp temporary teeth erupt around eighteen days. Shortly after, the dam's enthusiasm for round-the-clock nursing and maid service ebbs.

About this time, the pups begin to relate to humans. They should be given plenty of gentle cuddling and attention. They might even become frisky with their littermates, showing their affection by mounting each other, no matter what the sex.

Keep track of weight (this is especially important with Toy breeds). Although it is not unusual for pups to have a slight weight loss, if it is more than ten percent of the birth weight or continues for more than one day, the pup must be given supplements. Birth weight should double in eight to ten days.

Put the weakest and smallest pups on the rear breasts with the most milk. The big guys take care of themselves.

Colostrum

The milk received from the dam within the first twenty-four to thirty-six hours is called colostrum; it contains the antibodies for the pups' immunity. The amount of immunity depends on the bitch's titer—how much protection she has. Titer is an unknown factor. The best process is to inoculate the dam prior to her breeding. Of course, if the dam has not been immunized, the colostrum won't protect her pups against those diseases.

It is vital for newborns to receive the colostrum. If the whelps do not suck on their own, squeeze it onto their tongue or give it by bottle or tube. The colostrum looks different from the later milk—it is thicker and yellowish.

If the pups do not receive the colostrum, they should be isolated from other dogs and people until inoculated. They have no immune system to respond to vaccine until the age of five to six weeks.

Hand-Feeding

Each feeding method has its own advantages and advocates. When nursing from the bottle, the pup makes the decision of how much it eats. This makes the pup work for its food (tube-feeding *can* produce lazy eaters). It satisfies the nursing instinct. It's the only method of choice if you're chicken.

Bottle-feeding is time-consuming, and you will spend most of your waking (and some of your sleeping) hours feeding and making formula.

If you choose this method, wiggle the nipple around when introducing the pups to it, encouraging them to nurse. Once they are accustomed to this strange mother, they become eager. They present quite a picture, curling their paws around the bottle.

The main advantages of tube-feeding are time efficiency and the ability to feed the puppy any amount you choose. Experts suggest the schedule shown in the table on the facing page.

Obtain a sixteen-inch soft rubber Number 8 French catheter and 35 cc syringe from your veterinarian. Sterilize the tube and syringe in antiseptic solution and rinse. Spread clean cooking oil around the inside of the syringe and plunger to lubricate.

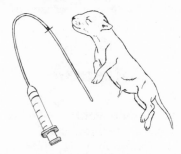

Measure the distance from the pup's mouth to the last rib and mark the tube, changing the distance as the puppy grows. Connect the syringe to the tube, insert the lower half of the tube into the formula, and pull back on the plunger, filling the syringe.

The easiest place to tube-feed is on the floor. Kneel, placing the pup on a towel between your legs. The pup should be facing in the same direction you are. Grasp the head lightly with your left hand and the tube with your right. Using your fingers at the corners of the mouth, gently force it open.

Place your index finger and thumb on the tube about three inches from the end. Insert the tube straight into the mouth toward the back of the throat, moving it over the tongue about two inches. Move your

Pup Weight		Formula Quantity		Feeding Schedule
lbs	**ozs**	**cc's***	**ozs**	**hours**
	3–7	1 per oz		3
	8	12		4
	10	15		4
	12	18		5
	14	21		5
1		24		5
1¼			1	5
1½			1⅓	5
1¾			1¾	6
2			2	6
2¼			2¼	6
2½			2½	6
3			3	6
		*(30 cc's = 1 oz)		

tube hand backward a couple of inches, pushing forward gently. Repeat in short strokes until the tube stops or the mark is reached.

When you are learning to tube-feed, the tendency is to work slowly, which may cause the puppy to gag. If the pup coughs or gags, or the tube stops short of its mark, pull the tube out partway and begin again.

The syringe can be placed on the floor during insertion of the tube. When the goal is reached, hold the syringe straight up, forcing the air to the upper part of the syringe, and depress the plunger.

Remove the tube quickly, and the procedure is over before either of you know it. If you give the pup too much, his safety valve will make him vomit or snuffle a bit out his nose.

Older pups may also be fed in this method if they are too ill or weak to eat. Care must be taken that they do not push the tube out. Healthy pups resist the tube after two weeks of age. Pan-feeding can be introduced at this age.

Dewclaws

We have five toes on each foot, and so do dogs—always on the front and sometimes on the rear. The teeny excuse for a fifth toe is located above the foot on the inside of the leg. According to the standards, some breeds should have the rear dewclaws removed, some are born without them, and others demand they be retained. Three—the Briard, the Beauceron, and the Great Pyrenees—require not one, but two rear dewclaws.

The front dewclaws are removed in most Sporting and Terrier breeds and in many others. This is done for grooming ease, a clean look to the front leg, and avoidance of accidents. If dewclaws are to be removed, the preferred time is between two and six days of age. If pups are older, it becomes a major operation. Veterinarians are so practiced in the removal that there is less chance of scarring.

A few experienced breeders handle removal themselves. The wound must be washed with antiseptic.

If not removed, dewclaws should be trimmed along with other nails. Otherwise, the nail curves inward, eventually piercing the leg. Dewclaws may also snag and tear, causing pain or hemorrhage.

Tail Docking

Several breeds have their tails docked (see Appendix 1: Breed Specifics). The surgery is done at two or three days of age, and should only be done by someone who is experienced and knowledgeable about Standard requirements. There are many variations in length, from the nub of the Schipperke, Old English Sheepdog, and Welsh Pembroke Corgi, to the longer span of the Viszla and Irish Terrier.

Although docking can be performed later, it changes from minor to major surgery. After one week of age, it must be done with anesthesia. If the tail was cut too short, that's the end of the tale. There are no tail transplants.

Newborn Eyes

Eyelids begin opening at about seven to fourteen days. One day a teensy crack appears, with a glint from the eye. Do not expose newly opened eyes to bright light. At three weeks, recognition begins.

If there is a stickiness around the eye, and the eye does not begin to open, wipe it gently with cotton soaked in warm water or with ophthalmic ointment.

An eye infection before the grand opening causes swelling around the eye. A vet must open the eyelid and drain the pus. Antibiotics are prescribed and the eye treated daily with medication. Action must be swift, or there may be corneal damage and loss of sight.

Runts

While one puppy may have a birth weight less than his siblings, a true "runt" is not as common as laymen believe. With proper care, the smallest pup can mature to become the largest. The runt of the litter is not necessarily the worst pup. This is especially true if all the other pups are oversized.

Sometimes, however, a puppy is greatly undersized in proportion to the rest of the litter. Positioning in the uterus, particularly in a large litter, can cause insufficient nourishment. The small pup may be the result of a much later breeding, though parturition has begun on the due date of the first breeding. Thus, matings five days or more apart can produce premature pups along with full-term ones. Poor nourishment of the bitch can also cause runts. Puppies that suffer congenital defects, such as heart disease, are usually born at average weight, losing ground neonatally.

Supplemental feeding helps in some circumstances. Most breeders do not want to give up easily on any puppies as long as they appear healthy and gain. There are too many stories of Best-in-Show winners or at least Kings-of-the-Household that are hale and hearty because their breeders exerted extra effort to aid survival.

If these methods do not help the little one catch up and thrive (as evidenced by daily weight gain), or if he loses or remains the same weight, there is probably an inborn defect. He should be euthanized before he starves or suffers. One breeder reported tube-feeding a pup for four weeks when he was still almost birth weight.

Colic

Colic may be caused by gas or by toxic milk. The affected pups cry, and have swollen abdomens and diarrhea. If the problem is discovered to be the mother's milk, the pups must be taken away and hand-fed by bottle or tube. Both mother and litter should receive antibiotics. A breeder of Bernese Mountain Dogs recommends Lactinex® for colicky pups.

Diarrhea

Antibiotics given to the pups or the dam can cause diarrhea as a side effect. If antibacterials must be given, don't wait for problems.

Lactobacillus, contained in uncultured yogurt, buttermilk, or Lactinex (from a health-food store), restores the natural intestinal bacteria that have been destroyed by the antibiotics. A little of any of these products never hurts.

Diarrhea in otherwise vigorous pups can also result from pigging out. Some mothers are very heavy milkers and greedy little ones eat more than they can digest. This disappears when they start walking and work off some flab.

Be on the alert for dehydration.

Dehydration

Dehydration evolves through infection or disease, and is caused directly by vomiting, diarrhea, fever, or failure to take nourishment. It is one of the most frequent causes of puppy death.

If a puppy is not eating eagerly or is sickly, beware of dehydration. The easiest way to discern the problem is to pluck the skin at the back of the dog's neck, then compare it to that of the littermates. Skin that springs back quickly has normal hydration, but if the skin is inelastic or returns slowly to position, the puppy is in trouble.

Fluids must be replaced by supplemental feeding, subcutaneous injections, or intravenous fluids at your vet's. If an older pup is still

eating, encourage him to consume more liquids by feeding him a salty food, such as beef bouillon.

Herpesvirus

There is no way of telling whether a dam is infected with herpesvirus. Although it is not fatal to adults, it does cause vaginitis. The virus is transmitted from the vaginal wall to the puppies during delivery and usually affects the whole litter. Since the bitch acquires immunity, her subsequent litters will not be affected.

The pups may suffer from yellow-green diarrhea and a drop in body temperature. This virus thrives in a subtemperature, about 95 degrees, and affects the kidneys and liver. Symptoms appear at about one to three weeks of age. Affected puppies suddenly become limp, refuse to nurse, and cry pitifully. Most die within twenty-four hours.

It may help to elevate the temperature of the pup to about 100°F (37.8°C). Give fluids to avoid dehydration.

Surviving pups sometimes have kidney failure between eight and ten months, due to viral damage. An experimental vaccine is being investigated.

Fading Puppy Syndrome

This phrase is a catchall name applied to puppies that begin fading and dying. Entire litters have succumbed within a day or two. Many times the cause is one of the above ailments (herpes, diarrhea, dehydration), and can also be the consequence of prematurity, genetic defects, stress, drugs, or disease. If the breeder is alert and prepared to combat the problem, or contacts the vet with the first symptoms, the litter can be saved.

At times, the malady can be reversed by giving the pups lactobacillus acidophilus, yogurt, or buttermilk. Work with your vet to find the reason for fading.

Hypoglycemia (Juvenile)

The symptoms of hypoglycemia (low blood sugar) are nervousness, staggering, falling down, or panting. A victim may shake or suffer convulsions. In mild cases, the symptoms may be reversed with a solution of glucose on the tongue every hour. Severe cases require glucose injections, given by your veterinarian.

Stress brings on such episodes, making this a severe problem in many Toy breeds as they are being weaned and going to new homes. By four months, the difficulty is usually outgrown.

Navel Ill

Bacteria can enter the navel opening, infecting any part of the body through the bloodstream. Joint, liver, and general infections have been known to develop in victims.

To prevent infection, treat the open cord with iodine immediately. Upon any indication of infection, bathe the area with Phisohex® and rinse twice daily. The infection must be treated with an antibiotic.

Swimmer

Most dogs are natural swimmers, but they shouldn't display this skill in the whelping box! A wide, flattened chest is easily detected, particularly by someone who has seen swimmers before. The puppy moves crabwise, with legs extended to the sides, moving in a breaststroke. Or its legs might extend straight back, with the pup seeming to move like a seal; thus the term "swimmer." This condition may develop because of improper footing, but it is also caused by weak muscles or deformed bones.

The legs do not function under the body, as the other pups' do, no matter how wobbly they are. If this condition is not corrected, the

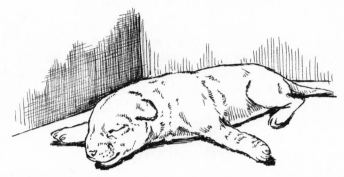

puppy will never walk normally, and in fact may be so crippled it must be euthanized. In addition, due to decreased chest capacity, swimmers may suffer from difficult breathing and heart failure.

Successful treatments offered by breeders include handling the puppy daily, gently pressing the soft, pliable ribs into the proper shape. Place rolled-up towels or rugs under nonskid flooring, forming hills and valleys to exercise the pup in the proper method of walking. It won't hurt the rest of the litter to build up muscle either!

Another recommendation is dangling the puppy in a tub of water. Ironically, swimming with proper use of the legs and expansion of the lungs aids correction of the swimmer syndrome. Attempt to keep the puppy lying on his side rather than on his tummy, which flattens the chest even more. Every time you enter the room, place him on his side.

In severe cases, the pup should be taped around the front elbows, pulling the legs into the proper position. If the rear legs are also incorrectly positioned, they should be taped as well. Watch the puppy, so that it does not become overweight.

The earlier the treatment, the more likely the recovery. Some breeders also recommend large doses of vitamin C.

Fleas

There is nothing more pathetic than tiny puppies crawling with these parasites before they are even able to walk. Since most powders and sprays specify that they are to be used for pups over four weeks of age, it is not easy to eradicate the pests. Make sure the dam is free of fleas before breeding. Be sure to check infested pups for tapeworm, as fleas promote this other parasite.

Immediate Birth Defects

Examine all pups at birth for cleft palates, anasarca, hydrocephalus, and other obvious deformities, covered below. It is unproductive to save these pups. Most do not survive anyway. Others usually have to be euthanized eventually, so it is heartless to extend their suffering.

Hydrocephalus

In hydrocephalus, the dome of the skull is enlarged, accompanied by sunken eyes. This becomes more noticeable as time goes on. If the unfortunate pups who have this are not euthanized, the pressure on the brain causes retardation or death. Toy and brachycephalic breeds are afflicted with hydrocephalus more than others. (The importance of early diagnosis is illustrated by a dog who finished his Championship before the discovery of his deafness, caused by this condition.)

Schistosoma Reflexus

This is a developmental accident in which the intestines and other organs are not contained within the body cavity, but are on the outside. If not stillborn, these pups should be euthanized immediately.

Atresia Ani

A puppy suffering from this rare defect bloats and cries. The anal opening is either too small or entirely missing, or there is an internal gap between the bowel and the anus.

Cleft Palate/Harelip

A harelip is very obvious: the upper lip is split, sometimes through the nose. A cleft palate forms a crack in the roof of the mouth. Check the puppy by looking into the mouth and feeling the roof. Neither defect is unusual, and they often appear together.

Nursing is hampered by either condition; bubbles of milk appear from the nose. Death results from starvation or pneumonia when milk is inhaled into the lungs. Mild cases can be saved by tube-feeding.

Anasarca

Pups with this condition are aptly called "walrus pups" from their grossly swollen bodies. They often weigh three pounds plus at birth. It is a fatal condition.

Deafness/Blindness

Hereditary deafness is sometimes seen in white-headed dogs and merle-colored lines. Puppies may be tested starting at two weeks and weekly thereafter. Do not make noises that cause air waves (such as clapping of hands). Instead, bang a pan, ring bells, blow whistles.

Deaf pups do not move their ears, or bark as often or in the same way as do their littermates.

Early causes of blindness are congenital juvenile cataract and microphthalmia (very small eyes).

Culling

Any malformed pup, particularly with a life-threatening deformity, should be quickly and humanely put down. In addition, any pup that begins fading after birth and does not respond to special attention likely has an internal congenital defect and must be culled. You should take the defective pup away, distracting the dam with the rest. Some mothers seem to know when even one is in trouble. The vet can painlessly euthanize the pup to curtail suffering.

The law of nature—survival of the fittest—dictates that handicapped puppies do not survive. Such puppies need a great deal of care, time, and often, money to help them. It is difficult to find homes that are willing to adopt these cases. Unless you are willing to raise the pups in comfort, it is most humane to euthanize them.

Sometimes the mother culls a puppy herself, by repeatedly rejecting or removing a sickly pup or one that is subnormal in temperature. In this case, warm the puppy. If the mother does not accept her pup after survival techniques are used, take it to the vet for an exam. A small dose of glucose solution (see Lifeguard Techniques, in Chapter 8) often tips the odds, and the dam will then accept her fledgling.

Show breeders sometimes choose to cull puppies that have disqualifying Standard faults but are otherwise healthy. Some do not allow a bitch to care for too large a litter, though most breeders agree they would have difficulty selecting which pup is to live and which is to die. If they are removed from the gene pool, they are effectively culled. "Culling" does not always mean killing—the imperfect but healthy pups can be given away unregistered or sold on neuter/spay contract.

11. TOT TO TEEN

During the stage from four to eight weeks of age, all your hard work begins to pay bonuses. Watching the pups bounce and roll across your lawn makes you keenly aware of what you have accomplished. You brought these bouncy, bubbly beings to life with your planning and the bitch's cooperation. You begin to realize what responsibility you have brought on yourself. Perhaps more than you bargained for. But you've gotten it whether you want it or not, and you'd better back up the last four weeks of hard work with another month of the same.

During this time, pups are awake more and play, trying out their toddling legs and their barks. Individual characteristics emerge at this age. One is rowdy, one is sweet, another is unsure. Some personality molding can be helpful, such as encouraging and cheering on the hesitant; gently reprimanding the impatient loudmouth; and cuddling the underdog.

The pecking order is being established; pups enter into their tough fights, and the more timid littermates submit to the more dominant ones. One Kerry Blue Terrier enthusiast always separates her pups by eight or ten weeks to prevent fighting, thus avoiding serious personality problems.

About this time, the dam ends her latrine duties along with weaning—though a few continue until their charges are six months or more. To make things easier for yourself, promote cleanliness.

As soon as the puppies' eyes are open and they are trying out their jelly legs, divide the box into livingroom and bathroom quarters. Put newspaper, sawdust, or a similar product at one end of the box. The water and food bowls should be placed in that area. As the pups charge toward the attractions, they stop to relieve themselves. Since dogs are naturally clean animals, they prefer not to dirty their sleeping area.

Introduction to a collar and leash is an added bonus for the buyer. While the puppies need not be little robots, it is pleasant when the new owner does not have to drag them off gagging and screeching. Teach them to stand/stay from five weeks of age, starting with just a split second, followed by delighted crows and hugs on your part, and proud kisses on the part of the pup. Lengthen the time daily, and soon you have a pup who does not act like an idiot on his first trip to the vet. Manners are not only for show dogs.

Socializing is extremely important, in fact vital, during the eight-to-ten-week period. Traumatic events during this time can have a long-term effect. Conversely, a wide variety of positive experiences helps pups cope for a lifetime.

Juvenile Vaginitis

A slight discharge of mucoid material, usually tinted yellow, is not unusual in prepubertal bitches, even in the whelping box. They may lick frequently, cleaning themselves and attempting to alleviate the irritation. They can be attractive to males, especially inexperienced young males.

These cases invariably clear up with the onset of the first season, with or without treatment. These are not of the serious nature that a bloody pus discharge would be in a postadolescent bitch. The infection is confined to the vaginal area. If the irritation is pronounced or if your vet is concerned about the bladder being involved, localized treatment is initiated. If it should recur after the first season, a more aggressive treatment can be attempted.

Weaning

Bitches have been observed standing with clenched jaws as three-month-old puppies hang on their shriveled teats. Of course, there are also those who would just as soon turn the whole thing over to you at birth. Now and then a dam weans the litter by herself. A few just kiss them all good-bye, leave the box, and never look back. Others regurgitate their meals, as wild dogs do, and the puppies dive in with zest. If mama has this tendency, begin weaning in earnest, as she also needs the nutrition of her meals.

Weaning begins at about three weeks and is completed by five to seven weeks. Mix rice baby cereal with a bit of milk and yogurt, making it runny enough for the puppies to lap. Some dive in eagerly, and others have to be coaxed. Nudge their noses into the cereal to stir interest. At the same time, reduce the mother's food and liquids.

Later, meals can be supplemented with egg yolks, scrambled eggs, baby meat, or crumbled hamburger. Don't accustom them to gourmet food, but do offer a menu tempting enough to whet their appetites.

Dog food crumbled finely in the blender is soon substituted for the cereal. Before long, your food bill swells, along with their tummies.

Feed the puppies four times a day by five weeks, and begin weaning mama away from the litter. Let her feed and clean the brood overnight for three days, then every other night for two more days. At that time, keep her out of the litterbox for three complete days. This process dries her up gradually and is easier on everyone than a swift separation.

After complete weaning, allow the mother to play with her youngsters if she wishes. Don't be surprised if she doesn't. Most dams wear a martyred look. Some, however, continue the education of their brood. Use discretion, as the dam may become too rough in discipline, and then accidents happen. Two weeks after weaning, the shedding process begins. Just about the time when buyers come to look at the pups and ask to see the dam, she will look like a bag lady, with shriveled teats and a shabby coat.

Grooming

Brushing, particularly in long-haired breeds, should be introduced at four or five weeks, starting with just a couple of strokes and increasing daily. Early adjustment at just six weeks to electric clippers and trimming is suggested by Cocker and Poodle fanciers. The sooner the puppies learn their lot in life, the easier it is for both owner and pet.

When pan-feeding begins, mothers stop grooming, and the chore falls to the breeder. The dam's work ends and she withdraws to the sofa for a well-earned rest. Feeding is sloppy, and so are puppies. They must be toweled clean and dried.

Worming

A stool sample should be routinely examined at four weeks of age, or earlier if symptoms warrant. If positive, medication obtained from the vet is used at about five weeks and again at eight weeks, before they go to their new homes.

To skimp on worming is a false economy. Wormy pups are unattractive and listless. They have dull coats and loose stools. The purchase price of such unappealing youngsters is less than those that are sparkling with good health.

Run a stool test to see which parasite is being harbored. No deworming agent kills every worm. The puppies must be weighed before dosing. The medications are toxic and overdosing can cause illness or death. Of course, if the puppies are not infested, it is unnecessary—even detrimental—to worm.

Use products made only for young puppies. Products should not be combined, since they are toxic and combinations could be lethal to more than the parasites.

Youngsters with heavy infestations are potbellied, yet thin around the ribs and hipbones. There may be diarrhea. Although worms seldom show in stools at this age, they may appear by eight weeks.

Roundworms commonly plague puppies. The more serious hookworm can be fatal. Be alert for signs of anemia—white gums, listlessness, or bloody stools. Severe anemia requires blood transfusions.

In addition to internal parasites, pups can be bothered by external parasites, most commonly fleas. Fleas carry tapeworm larvae.

Coccidiosis

The stigma of an unclean kennel should not prevent the breeder from seeking help if an outbreak of coccidiosis occurs. Most active breeders eventually have litters that suffer from this malady. The parasite may be carried in from the outside world by people or dogs and is also transmitted by flies. The dam could be a carrier if she herself had coccidiosis.

Stress activates the coccidia parasites. This culprit strikes at about six to eight weeks—after weaning or upon arrival at a new home. Oocysts, the immature form of coccidia, show up in a stool sample. Symptoms are diarrhea, loss of appetite, and listlessness. Blood appears in the stools when the intestines become irritated. If neglected, the illness leads to dehydration. Recovery is quick and treatment simple. Diarrhea should be curbed at the same time with kaolin-pectin mixtures. Treatment should involve the whole litter. If one has it, the others soon will. Ignoring the situation can cause debilitation of the pups, and even death.

Once coccidia are on your grounds, they are difficult to eradicate. The premises must be thoroughly disinfected. Although there are many expensive disinfectants, bleach works as well as anything.

Immunizations

Discuss a schedule for inoculations with your vet. Many dog breeders give DHLP (distemper, hepatitis, leptospirosis, and parainfluenza) vaccines at six and twelve weeks. Others prefer half doses, especially for tiny Toys, at six and nine weeks, followed by an adult shot at twelve weeks. Parvo vaccine is most often given at six, nine, twelve, and sixteen weeks. The stated preference is modified live vaccine.

A rabies shot is given between four and six months. Even if it is not required by your state, professionalism demands protection of puppies against all diseases. A complete record of all vaccines and dates given should be noted and given to the buyers.

Umbilical Hernia

If your puppy has an "outie," a lump appearing at the navel, he has an umbilical hernia. Although this can be corrected surgically in a fairly simple procedure, it is not always necessary to do so.

Hernias may be inherited or developed. The tissues surrounding the umbilical area may be genetically weak, causing the hernia. A

hereditary predisposition can be determined by investigating the pups of an affected dam. The dam or an excited owner pulling on the cord at birth can lead to an umbilical hernia, even if there is no inherited tendency.

Often the hernia becomes smaller as the puppy grows. It seldom causes difficulty. Before breeding a bitch, an examination of its severity should be conducted.

Puppy Strangles

Severe staphylococcus infections can occur in pups less than sixteen weeks old. The first signs may be infected pimples, especially around the head. This quickly progresses to grossly swollen lips, ears, eyelids, and lymph nodes, giving the appearance of mumps.

Although medically termed juvenile pyoderma, the lay term of "strangles" is apropos, referring to the pressure of the enlarged neck lymph nodes. These nodes may abscess and drain pus.

Researchers feel that the cause of this condition is a hypersensitivity to the staph bacteria. Thus it may not affect all pups in a litter. Probably, the sensitivity theory also explains why cortisones combined with the appropriate antibiotic often allow a dramatic recovery.

Diaper Rash

Impetigo appears on puppies in the form of pimples or red sores filled with pus. Lesions erupting on the belly or groin area are started by urine irritation.

Keep the area clean by washing daily with warm water and a soap containing hexachlorophene, such as Phisohex.® Rinse well. These staphylococcus infections require treatment with antibiotics. Keep the kennel and bedding clean.

Descension of Testicles

All males should have two testicles present in the scrotum. Most breeders wait as eagerly for their descent as for the landing of a spaceship. Even in the large breeds, the testicles are as tiny as BB's, and it takes a practiced hand to feel them at an early age. Although the testes are developed at birth, many do not descend into the sac until the pups are several weeks old.

The age at which descent occurs varies according to breeds and lines. Many authorities state that they are unlikely to descend after six months. Most owners admit that they become very, very nervous after ten weeks. There is more hope when the testicle can be felt in the tract. Descent has been noted as late as one year. Late descent, however, is enough to cause elimination of the dog and the tendency from many breeding programs.

Of course, all breeders agree that the pup that does not have both testicles present and accounted for is invariably, according to Murphy's Law, the best pup in the litter, if not in the history of his kennel. There is probably no greater anticipation among breeders. It ranks with the World Series and the Super Bowl.

One testicle in the sac is commonly referred to as monorchidism, but is medically termed unilateral cryptorchidism. A dog with no descended testicles is called cryptorchid (bilateral cryptorchid). It makes no difference. One testicle makes it closer, but still no cigar.

AKC regulations state that a dog must be entire to be shown in the breed ring. Monorchidism has been considered just another fault in some countries. Since 1959, monorchids may not compete in the breed ring in Great Britain. It is common in all breeds and appears often enough without perpetuating the fault by breeding affected animals. A bilateral cryptorchid is sterile, since the testicles remain inside the body, and body heat is not conducive to sperm formation.

Although some breeders attempt descension with testosterone, the probability of success is remote. In fact, testosterone or FSH may be counterproductive if done too early.

An incomplete male should not be bred, and neutering eliminates any "accidents." Testicles retained in the body invite tumors, and neutering precludes this possibility.

Puppies sometimes retract their testicles if they are nervous, upset, or entered in a match show (just to embarrass their owner). This is a toddler trait. By the time the pup reaches four months or thereabouts, the testicles are too large to recede into the body cavity. Rarely, a pup draws up a testicle permanently.

Do not examine daily. Too much handling draws attention to the area, and nervous puppies pull up testicles. Check the pups at about six weeks when the testicles become large enough to be felt with ease. Once the puppy enters training, if he is to be shown, he should become accustomed to having people handle his private parts.

Testicles should be rechecked prior to sale. Though most pet buyers do not care whether the dog has both testicles, they should be informed of the fact, and you should suggest that the dog be neutered.

Ear Cropping

Like tail docking and dewclaw removal, this surgery has become cosmetic rather than utilitarian. Originally, all the shortening, removing, and tailoring was performed so that the dog could better fulfill its lot in life—fighting, hunting, guarding—without ripping off part of its anatomy.

Today we have become accustomed to seeing only short tails on Cocker Spaniels, cropped ears on Doberman Pinschers, and clean legs with dewclaws removed on Chesapeake Bay Retrievers. Anything else looks odd to us, at least in this country. Several other countries have banned cosmetic surgery.

Ear surgery is major and must be done under general anesthetic. The age at which surgery is performed and the shape and length of the ears are dictated by the breeds, but most operations are advised between six to ten weeks. If done later, it is more traumatic for the dog and there is less chance of success.

Seek advice on choosing a veterinarian who is practiced in performing these surgeries. Ask the breeder from whom you bought your dog or a breeder at a show. Styles are varied from breed to breed and ear fashions, like hemlines, change over the years.

Oversize

Studies show that a pup weighing twenty pounds at the age of eight weeks makes an ideal candidate for hip dysplasia. This is not a blanket diagnosis, obviously, but rather a warning to those who tend to think bigger is better. Oversize puppies increase the likelihood of hip malformation even though the pup's genes may be poised to go in either direction.

Some of the giant breeds—Great Danes, Newfoundlands, Saint Bernards, and others—routinely weigh over twenty pounds at eight weeks, and these breeds also have a higher percentage of HD. Breeders need not underfeed a pup either, risking malnutrition, but puppies should not become obese or be oversupplemented. Feeding should correspond to bone structure.

Puppies are normally roly-poly until six weeks, when they begin to slim naturally into minature adults. While they should never be bony, obesity can cause problems in later life. Giant breeds are actually safer being lean during youth.

Hermaphrodites

"Hermaphrodite" means more than bisexual. It means actually possessing the organs of both sexes. True hermaphrodites that contain testicular and ovarian tissue—sometimes in the same organ—are extremely rare. They are always sterile. This condition can only be determined by doing a biopsy. In most cases, the owner simply believes the dog is unproductive. The pseudo-hermaphrodite possesses external genitalia of both sexes.

Such cases have been confirmed by a vet who noted testicles under the skin on a bitch anesthetized for ear cropping, and by a breeder who recorded two incidents of hermaphrodites, from a half-brother/ sister breeding. In one case, the pup appeared normal when sold. At five months, the vulva was enlarged, with a wartlike growth inside that developed into a definite penis. This pup also developed doggy characteristics. The second showed her condition at weaning age. They are both leading normal, healthy lives in other respects.

Esophagus

Esophagus abnormalities begin to appear at weaning. The dog cannot keep down its food and repeatedly regurgitates. When the food finally liquefies, it stays down.

Aortic arch anomalies are arteries that constrict the esophagus and form a pocket, causing spontaneous vomiting. Achalasia is another form in which the entire esophagus is dilated. Pyloric stenosis (stomach valve spasms) causes projectile vomiting.

Surgery may help, but severe cases are usually euthanized. Diagnosis is made by barium X ray.

In the situation where a puppy is already established in a home as a beloved pet, the symptoms can be eased by elevating the food bowl. The food slides down the esophagus more easily than when feeding at ground level, as dogs usually do.

Congenital Heart Disease

Puppies with heart disease often exhibit breathing difficulties and intolerance to exercise. Breathing is rapid and labored, with short rather than deep breaths. This is easy to spy, because when breathing is normal, you do not notice it. Remember your last cold?

There may be coughing, and in severe cases the pups are blue. When the puppy is picked up, the heartbeat might be felt through the chest.

Before selling, puppies should have a veterinary exam, including the heart. The healthy heart beat is a strong LUB-DUB, LUB-DUB. A defect shows up as a rapid or disrupted rhythm. A WHOOOOOSH may be heard.

Some heart defects are surgically correctable, and dogs can live with minor defects, but affected dogs should never be bred. Even if the ailment is not hereditary, the stress of pregnancy and raising pups is too much for a dog that is not in peak condition.

Patella

Patellar problems plague small breeds the way hip dysplasia is a curse of larger dogs. Both defects appear in nearly all breeds, but slipped kneecaps happen more frequently in small dogs.

Patellar luxation is nearly always a hereditary crippler. Diagnosis is made by palpation at weaning. Corrective surgery is extensive, and is only practical when the value is sentimental.

Entropion/Ectropion

Dogs suffering from entropion have lower eyelids that roll inward, causing the lashes to rub the eyeball. Symptoms are squinting, irritation, and tearing. Dogs with loose facial skin and small, deep-set eyes seem prone to this weakness. The condition is hereditary. Severe cases must be surgically corrected. The irritation may lead to corneal damage and eventual blindness.

The opposite condition is ectropion, where the eyelid rolls outward. The sagging eyelid allows dust and dirt to lodge in the eyelid, causing constant irritation, redness, and mattering. This can be controlled by frequent and careful eye care. Washes and ointments offer some ease.

Temperament

Since you have chosen breeding partners that have good temperaments, their puppies should demonstrate the same quality. However, there are black sheep in even the best of families. A stable temperament typical of the breed should be encouraged in every way.

Puppies need to be handled frequently by family members. Allow the pups to play gently with older dogs that possess the proper temperament. When the litter is old enough to have resistance to disease, invite other people to come and play with them. Bring them to training classes. Owners of herding dogs endorse socialization as particularly important for their chosen breeds.

Cheer on desired activities and actions—curiosity, wagging tails, and boldness, for example. Discipline bad habits by raising your voice, clapping hands sharply while saying, "NO!" and pinning them to the canvas as you've seen the mother do. Build up confidence by giving plenty of human contact to pups that are unsure, praising them for each step forward, and saying, "GOOOOOOD, PUPPY!" when they try.

When prospective buyers come, find out what kind of home life they have and what kind of personality they prefer. Point out the pups that are mischievous or obedient or docile.

Evaluation

If you are a show devotee yourself and wish to save a couple of puppies for show purposes, study their movements and attitude from the earliest moments. A dog that is correctly built also moves properly. Look for the pup that has the world by the tail, rather than the other way around.

An ideally built dog that has a lackadaisical manner will have a difficult time in the ring, although it could produce well. A dog that has a minor fault or two but does not know it himself could run rings around the others. Top-quality show animals are rare. There are many that come close, but the dog (or bitch) that possesses a beautiful body along with a Muhammad Ali manner is a dog that is almost impossible to beat.

Look for the pup that is one step closer to the ideal than its parents. If you're keeping it, that pup will bring your kennel closer to its goals. If you're selling it, the buyer will always remember the breeder who sold him such a fine animal. The reverse, of course, is even more true. Buyers never forget being stung.

Ethics in Raising and Selling

Give the dam and pups every advantage in health care.

Treat all puppies equally, not just those you are keeping or those marked for show homes.

Screen your buyers to obtain only the best homes for your pups.

Observe your pups, and select only the best pets for each buyer.

Clean puppies make clean adults.

Be honest in your observations. Tell buyers that a puppy is a monorchid, has a bad bite, or an improper coat. Most people who are looking for a pet to love won't care. But they certainly will care if they find out about the fault from someone else.

Do not mislead buyers into thinking they can finish a Championship on a mediocre pup.

Stand behind your guarantees.

If situations change and the dog must be sold, help the buyer to find a good home.

Study your breed, and always strive for improvement.

There is no greater feeling than buyers calling to tell you how delighted they are with their pup, and no gut ache more painful than hearing a buyer insinuate that it's your fault the dog has destroyed the house or, worse yet, has an incurable disease.

Bittersweet

You've heard them all. You've got to take the bad with the good. Every cloud has a silver lining. If you didn't have sorrow, you couldn't know joy. Gray skies will turn to blue. April showers bring

May flowers. There's always somebody worse off. Make lemonade out of lemons.

Although many of the lemons have been presented in these chapters, you may never experience them. If you do, perhaps you will overcome them.

Dog breeding is a bittersweet experience. If you're a true dog lover, the sweet far outweighs the bitter.

Appendix

APPENDIX

Breed Specifics and Predispositions

We have listed all genetic conditions reported from our extensive search of reference material and breeders' and veterinarians' records. Some conditions are highly suggestive of being inherited and others are definitely proven to be. Many conditions are very rare; others occur with frequency. The actual numbers are impossible to obtain.

If you own a Beagle or are considering the purchase of one, your dog will never suffer all, or even most, of the conditions listed. The same is true of any breed. The chances of the disorders occurring are greater in some breeds than in others. Many of the genetic disorders make random appearances in other breeds as well. For instance, hip dysplasia has been found in every breed except the racing Greyhound.

Our survey participants are veterans in canine midwifery. Years of research and expertise have yielded their answers to the questions that follow and their experiences related in the text itself.

The breeds given in this appendix represent the purebreds found in North America.

Note that where categories are eliminated, they are not applicable to the particular breed.

Key:

No. BREED
A. List any idiosyncrasies apparent in females of your breed during puberty, breeding, or pregnancy.
B. List those exhibited by males.
C. Average litter size.
D. Average birth weight in ounces.
E. Give information on whelping and motherhood.
F. Give details on dewclaws.
G. Give details on docking tails.
H. Give details on cropping or setting ears.
I. List deviations from the Standards, or required "oddities" (e.g., underbite).
J. Reported genetic disorders.

1. AFFENPINSCHER
A. Normal.
B. Normal, eager breeder.
C. Two to four.
D. Three to five.
E. Breeches may be a problem due to large head size; cesarean may be necessary.
F. All removed.
G. Docked near body, leave one third.
H. Cropped at twelve to sixteen weeks, short with bell.
J. Anasarca*, aseptic necrosis of femoral head, corneal ulcer, patellar luxation, cryptorchidism, elongated soft palate, retained puppy teeth, dermoid cyst, schistosoma reflexus.

2. AFGHAN HOUND
A. Puberty can be as late as two years. Thrash, scream, and/or bite during breedings. Owners warn that they should never breed unattended.
B. Puberty often not until eighteen to twenty-four months. Normal breeders.
C. Seven.
D. Ten to eighteen.
E. Large litters, may be slow but normal. Scream, can be lazy. If overassisted, may let you do it all.
F. Remove dewclaws.
I. Light eyes, white on head (disqualifying).
J. Underbites, cataracts—juvenile, elbow-joint deformity, hip dysplasia, degener-ative myelopathy, chronic pancreatitis, corneal dystrophy, hypersensitivity to some insecticides and anesthesias, von Willebrand's disease.

3. AIREDALE
A. Puberty—fifteen months. Normal, eager breeders, sometimes muzzle.
B. Normal.
C. Eight to twelve.
D. Twelve to fifteen.
E. Dig and nest vigorously. Small litters sometimes cause problems. Good mothers.
F. Remove rear dewclaws if present.
G. Leave two thirds of tail; upright tail should reach height of top of head.
H. Set ears during teething.
I. Soft coats, drop ears.
J. Cerebellar hypoplasia, hypothyoidism, spondylosis deformans, pyometra, hindquarter trembling, ataxia, umbilical hernias, bad bites (lower jaw grows very late; overbites often correct), Factor IX deficiency, von Willebrand's disease.

4. AKBASH DOG
A. Cycle once a year.
B. Normal; early puberty, but late maturity.
C. Eight.
D. Thirty to thirty-six.
E. Free whelpers, good mothers.

*For a definition of this and other terms used in this survey, see Glossary, which begins on page 187.

F. Singles or doubles common in back—don't remove.

H. Cropped in Turkey, but not in USA.

J. Enostosis, hypertrophic osteodystrophy.

5. AKITA

A. False seasons common.

B. Very discriminating, only interested on right day— may have to fall in love!

C. Six to ten.

D. Sixteen to twenty-four.

E. Often no outward signs of pregnancy. Normal, but slow; long intervals between pups. Occasional eclampsia. Super mothers.

F. Remove rear dewclaws if present.

H. Tape ears if not up by four months.

I. Long coats, large ear with heavy leather.

J. Hip dysplasia, entropion, retinal atrophy—general progressive, hypothyroidism, increased sensitivity to anesthesia, vestibular disorder.

6. ALASKAN MALAMUTE

A. Early puberty, normal breeder.

B. Easy breeder—likes to play first.

C. Six to eight.

D. Twelve to twenty-two.

E. Free whelpers, good mothers.

F. Remove rear if present.

I. Poor pigment.

J. Hip dysplasia, chondrodysplasia, macrocytic anemia, renal cortical hypoplasia, hypothyroidism, cataract—

juvenile, patent ductus arteriosus, hemeralopia, enchondromatosis, factor VII deficiency, factor VIII deficiency, missing teeth, bad bites, missing vertebra in tail, Factor IX deficiency.

7. AMERICAN ESKIMO (MINATURE AND STANDARD)

A. Normal.

B. Normal.

C. Eight.

D. Sixteen.

E. Free whelpers; good, protective mothers.

F. Rears removed.

I. Rear dewclaws.

J. None reported.

8. AMERICAN FOXHOUND

A. Normal.

B. Normal.

C. Eight.

D. Sixteen.

E. Almost no problems; litters may be so large that the dam may lie on the pups or have trouble feeding all of them.

F. Remove all.

J. Osteochondrosis of spine, thrombocytopathy, deafness, cryptorchidism.

9. AMERICAN STAFFORDSHIRE TERRIER

A. Aggressive breeders.

B. Eager, sometimes aggressive.

C. Seven to eight.

D. Twelve.

E. Free whelpers, good mothers.

F. Remove all.

H. Cropped short and straight (no curve).

9. AMERICAN STAFFORD-
SHIRE TERRIER (*cont.*)
I. Crooked or partially missing tails.
J. Craniomandibular osteopathy, cervical vertebral instability, cleft palate, hip dysplasia, cataract—bilateral,
bad bites, cryptorchidism.

10. AMERICAN WATER
SPANIEL
A. Normal.
B. Normal.
C. Six to eight.
D. Eight to ten.
E. Free whelpers, nervous
mothers if other dogs
around.
F. Remove all.
I. Yellow eyes, poor coats
(nonmarcelled).
J. Hermaphrodites, hip dys-
plasia, epilepsy, retinal
atrophy—progressive.

11. ANATOLIAN SHEPHERD
A. Late ovulation, often difficult
to breed.
B. Normal.
C. Eight to ten.
D. Sixteen to twenty-four.
E. Free whelpers, good
mothers.
F. Rear removed.
H. Cropped in Turkey.
J. Entropion, hip dysplasia,
hypersensitivity to anes-
thesia and insecticide.

12. AUSTRALIAN CATTLE
DOG
A. Normal.
B. Normal, eager.
C. Three to six.
D. Twelve to sixteen.
E. Free whelpers, don't inter-
fere. Note: pups are born

white, roaning comes in
later.
F. Remove only rear if
present.
I. Body patches of color.
J. Deafness.

13. AUSTRALIAN SHEPHERD
A. Normal.
B. Normal, although some
lines lack libido.
C. Five to ten.
D. Eight to sixteen.
E. Good mothers, free
whelpers.
F. Remove all.
G. Docked quite short, leaving
just a stub if not born
tailless.
J. Spina bifida, poor temperament, cleft palate, hip dysplasia, retinal atrophy,
cataracts—juvenile, microphthalmia, bad bites, epilepsy, deafness.

14. AUSTRALIAN TERRIER
A. Normal.
B. Normal, eager.
C. Four to five.
D. Five to seven.
E. Easy whelpers, fifty-nine to
sixty-one days.
F. Remove all.
G. Dock, leaving a generous
two fifths.
H. Clip hair or tape if not up
by three months.
J. Diabetes mellitus, aseptic
necrosis of the femoral
head, cryptorchidism, atop-
tic dermatitis, cleft palates.

15. BASENJI
A. One heat per year (in fall),
lasts four weeks.
B. Normal.
C. Five to six.

D. Six to eight.
E. Easy whelpers, good mothers.
F. Remove all.
J. Pyruvate kinase deficiency, Fanconi syndrome, coliform enteritis, persistent pupillary membrane, corneal leukoma, malabsorption syndrome, bad bites, inguinal and umbilical hernias, octic disc coloboma.

16. BASSET HOUND
A. Normal, but often use breeding rack due to shape.
B. Difficult because of size and weight, often AI.
C. Eight to nine.
D. Eight to sixteen.
E. Can be slow whelpers with large litters, occasional cesareans. X-ray since hard to tell when done.
F. Remove all.
I. Long coats.
J. Bad bites, ectropion, corneal dermoid cyst, aggressive temperaments, osteochondritis dessicans, radius curvus, patellar luxation, glaucoma—primary, inguinal hernia, ununited anchoneal process, thrombopathia, deformed third cervical vertebra, cervical vertebral instability, achondroplasia, lens luxation, von Willebrand's disease.

17. BEAGLE
A. Normal.
B. Normal.
C. Five to six.
D. Eight to sixteen.
E. Thirteen inch variety often have pups that are too large to deliver naturally.

F. Remove all.
I. Short or crooked tails, size.
J. Bad bites, elongated soft palate, cryptorchidism, deafness, vestibular disorder, neuronal abiotrophy, cleft lip and palate, glaucoma-primary, retinal atrophy, ectasia, intervertebral disc disease, factor VII deficiency, factor VIII deficiency, renal cortical hypoplasia, otocephalic syndrome, cutaneous asthenia, globoid cell leukodystrophy, Lafora's disease, unilateral kidney aplasia, mononephrosis, gangliosidosis, epilepsy, pyruvate kinase deficiency, epiphyseal dysplasia, spina bifida, pulmonic stenosis, cataract—unilateral, atopic dermatitis, cataract—with microphthalmia, retinal dysplasia.

18. BEARDED COLLIE
A. May cycle longer than six months, eight to twelve not uncommon. Maidens often fight deflowering. Some inverted vulvas.
B. Very lusty, mount at three weeks in whelping box. Sometimes overexcited, with poor aim. Some sterility.
C. Seven.
D. Ten to twelve.
E. First-timer may be vocal with first pup. Free whelpers but large litters and long bodies can make aiding necessary with first pups.
F. Removal of front optional.
I. Mismarks, smooth or

18. BEARDED COLLIE (*cont.*)
woolly coats, fading pigment (nose and eye rims).
J. Bad bites, nasal solar dermatitis, hip dysplasia, retinal atrophy, subaortic stenosis, epilepsy, cleft palates, persistent pupillary membrane, cystitis.

19. BEAUCERON
A. Normal.
B. Normal, eager.
C. Ten.
D. Fourteen to eighteen.
E. Free whelpers, good mothers.
F. Double rear dewclaws required.
H. Cropped—"rustic" (short and wide) or "elegant" (as pet Dobe).
J. Tough working stock, very few problems.

20. BEDLINGTON TERRIER
A. Normal, but long intervals.
B. Normal.
C. Four to six.
D. Six.
E. Good mothers, often injure pups' tails, which are very long.
F. Remove all.
J. Missing canine teeth, distichiasis, retinal dysplasia, renal cortical hypoplasia, copper toxicosis, osteogenesis imperfecta, lacrimal duct atresia.

21. BELGIAN MALINOIS
A. Normal.
B. Normal.
C. Eight to eleven.
D. Twelve to thirteen.
E. Easy whelpers (pups are born black and lighten with age); pups need socialization.
H. Tape if not up by twelve weeks.
J. Bad bites, shyness, hip dysplasia, epilepsy, hypothyroidism.

22. BELGIAN SHEEPDOG
A. Normal.
B. Good, eager.
C. Eight to eleven.
D. Twelve to thirteen.
E. Easy whelpers, good mothers. Pups need socialization.
F. Remove all.
H. Tape if not up by twelve weeks.
I. Silver coat (not silver muzzles).
J. Bad bites, shyness, congenital nystagmus, hip dysplasia, hypothyroidism, epilepsy, hypersensitivity to barbiturates.

23. BELGIAN TERVUREN
A. Normal.
B. Slow to mature.
C. Eight to eleven.
D. Twelve to thirteen.
E. Easy whelpers (pups are born black and lighten with age). Pups need socialization.
H. Tape if not up by twelve weeks.
J. Bad bites, shyness, epilepsy, hypothyroidism, hip dysplasia.

24. BERNESE MOUNTAIN DOG
A. Regular cyclers, but notoriously hard to settle.
B. Some uninterested.
C. Eight to ten.
D. Sixteen to twenty-four.

E. Cesareans common; slow whelpers. If more than one hour between pups, intervene with POP or surgery. Low birth survival drive, "dishrag" pups.

F. Remove all, including extra rear toe.

I. Mismarks, blue or partially blue eyes.

J. Bad bites, hip dysplasia, osteochondritis dessicans, cleft palates, retinal atrophy—generalized progressive, fragmented coronoid process.

25. BICHON FRISE

A. Cycle irregularly, silent heats, annular rings common.

B. Normal, very macho.

C. Four to five.

D. Three and one half to four.

E. Very sensitive to pain, but usually OK. May need manual or surgical assistance.

F. Remove all.

I. Ten percent color OK by Standard.

J. Bad teeth with age, patellar luxation, epilepsy, hip dysplasia, Factor IX deficiency.

26. BLACK AND TAN COONHOUND

A. Normal.

B. Normal.

C. Seven to ten.

D. Twelve to sixteen.

E. Free whelpers, good mothers.

F. Removal optional.

J. Ectropion, hip dysplasia, factor IX deficiency.

27. BLOODHOUND

A. Flag throughout season, resorptions common, hard to diagnose pregnancy.

B. Lazy, careless breeders, AI's common.

C. Seven to eight.

D. Sixteen to eighteen.

E. Long, slow deliveries with retained placentas; planned cesareans common. A few are poor mothers. Pups not hardy; don't handle them frequently.

F. Removal optional.

I. Coat too fine.

J. Bad bites, ectropion, cryptorchidism, hip dysplasia, ununited anchoneal process, gastric torsion, bad temperaments, entropion, Stockard's paralysis, primary uterine enertia.

28. BORDER COLLIE

A. Normal.

B. Normal.

C. Five to eight.

D. Sixteen.

E. Easy whelpers.

J. Bad bites, cryptorchidism, retinal atrophy—central progressive, corneal dystrophy, osteochondritis dessicans, deafness, lens luxation.

29. BORDER TERRIER

A. Can have silent heats and small tracts, but settle OK when bred.

B. Normal.

C. Four to seven.

D. Eight to twelve.

E. Usually free whelpers, but primary and secondary inertias (in large litters) do occur. May strongly resent owner's help.

29. BORDER TERRIER (*cont.*)
F. Remove all.
G. Born naturally short; do not cut.
I. Wry, kinked, or bob tails.
J. Cryptorchidism (may still descend at five to seven months), ventricular septal defects, hip dysplasia, primary uterine inertia, retinal atrophy.

30. BORZOI
A. Puberty often not till twenty-four mos. Settle better if bred more than once.
B. Puberty may be two yrs. Not very eager, easily discouraged. More than one person needed during tie.
C. Eight to ten.
D. Twelve to sixteen.
E. Free whelpers, but due to deep chest routine X ray necessary to be sure she's done. First pup may require assistance.
F. Remove all.
J. Missing premolars, gastric torsion, hypersensitivity to some anesthesias and insecticides, retinal dysplasia, retinal atrophy—generalized progressive, dysfibrinogenemia.

31. BOSTON TERRIER
A. Dry seasons, no swelling or bleeding even on right day. Bite, fight, and scream during breeding.
B. Lack of interest; use studs of other breeds to discern timing. Need help with breeding. Can become "stuck" with outside tie.
C. Three.
D. Seven to eight.

E. Primary inertia, too large pups, prolonged labor—frequent cesareans (ninety percent).
F. All removed (protects eyes).
G. Docked just to cover anus, if not born with natural "screw."
H. May be cropped for show appearance, but not necessary.
I. Mismarks, blue eyes.
J. Swimmers, "cocked" eyes, elongated soft palate, cherry eye, distichiasis, frequent vomiting, stenotic nares, wry mouth, anasarca, achalasia, patent ductus arteriosus, deafness, cataract—juvenile, hydrocephalus, cleft lip and palate, spina bifida, hyperadrenocorticism, persistent right aortic arch, aortic and carotid body tumors, patellar luxation, hemivertebra, craniomandibular osteopathy, mast cell tumor, pituitary tumor, oligodendroglioma, ataxia, achlorhydria.

32. BOUVIER DES FLANDRES
A. Irregular estrus, cystic ovaries, endometritis.
B. Normal.
C. One to fifteen.
D. Eight to twenty-four.
E. Dystocias common due to very large or very small litters.
F. Remove all.
G. Docked, leaving five eighths of an inch at three days.
H. Cropped, moderately short and straight with wide base.

J. Bad bites, cleft palate, gastric torsion, hypothyroidism.

33. BOXER
A. Late puberty, normal breeders. Vaginal hyperplasia and prolapse.
B. Normal.
C. Five to six.
D. Twenty.
E. Frequent cesareans since one or two pups are often much larger than the rest. Hard to tell when done. Rip rather than bite cord. Super mothers.
F. Remove all.
G. Docked, leaving three quarters of an inch at three days.
H. Cropped long and gracefully curved, with narrow base.
I. Whites and mismarks, unpigmented haw.
J. Cryptorchidism, "wet mouths," distichiasis, pyloric stenosis, subaortic stenosis, atrial septal defect, pulmonic stenosis, patellar luxation, corneal ulcer, gastric torsion, eosinophilic colitis, vaginal hyperplasia, hypersensitivity to anesthetics, factor II deficiency, intervertebral disc disease, spondylosis deformans, lymphadema, clefts of lip and palate, epilepsy, cystinuria, gingival hyperplasia, dermoid cyst, extra incisor, mast cell tumor, histiocytoma, oligodendroglioma, entropion, achalasia, calcium gout, elongated soft palate, tetralogy of Fallot, osteochondritis dessicans,

retinal atrophy-central progressive, von Willebrand's disease, hypoprothrombinemia, Factor VII deficiency.

34. BRIARD
A. Normal.
B. Normal.
C. Seven to thirteen.
D. Twelve.
E. Free whelpers.
F. Double in rear required. Can remove front dewclaws if preferred.
H. Cropped in short, tricornered shell cut at five to six weeks, glued to stand.
I. Yellow eye, white spot.
J. Hip dysplasia, gastric torsion, retinal atrophy-central progressive, hypothyroidism.

35. BRITTANY
A. Normal.
B. Normal.
C. Seven.
D. Six.
E. Free whelpers, good mothers.
F. Remove all.
G. Docked, leave width of finger (three quarters of an inch) at three days; some born tailless.
J. Cryptorchidism, bad bites, ectropion, hip dysplasia, factor VIII deficiency.

36. BRUSSELS GRIFFON
A. Normal, up to eighteen months before puberty.
B. Normal, very sexy.
C. Four to five.
D. Five to six.
E. Difficulties due to large-headed pups. Many prob-

36. BRUSSELS GRIFFON
    (cont.)
    lems in bitches under five
    pounds.
    F. Remove all.
    G. Docked, leaving one third.
    H. Cropped at three months,
       like Miniature Schnauzer
       ear, or left in natural drop.
    I. Chocolate or blue (disquali-
       fying colors), web feet.
    J. Brachury, urine-dribbler
       pups, hydrocephalus, hip
       dysplasia, patellar luxation,
       dislocated shoulder, disti-
       chiasis, wry mouth, cleft
       palates.

37. BULL TERRIER
    A. Easy breeders, though
       some very aggressive—put
       in breeding rack. May only
       cycle once a year.
    B. Normal, but too aggressive.
       A lot of AI's for handler
       convenience when both are
       very aggressive.
    C. Five to seven.
    D. Eleven to thirteen.
    E. Prolonged hard deliveries,
       may need oxytocin or cal-
       cium shot. Sixty percent ce-
       sareans, eclampsia fre-
       quent. Nervous mothers
       may mouth pups. Some
       pup mortality.
    F. Remove all.
    H. Do not crop. Tape if not up
       by ten weeks.
    J. Retained baby teeth, umbil-
       ical hernia, deafness, in-
       guinal hernia, mast cell
       tumor, clefts of lip and pal-
       ate, calcium gout.

38. BULLDOG
    A. Normal, but hard to detect
       day due to lack of tail.

    B. Due to body weight and
       shape, very few ties—hold
       together. AI's very
       common.
    C. Five.
    D. Fourteen.
    E. Under 10 percent free
       whelpers, poor muscle
       tone, small pelvis, large
       pups—planned cesareans
       common to normal. Can't
       reach vulva to clean or
       chew cord; good mothers.
    H. Glue ears back if not
       "rosed" by eight weeks.
    J. Vaginal hyperplasia, elon-
       gated soft palate, stenotic
       nares, loose shoulders, ec-
       tropion, corneal dermoid
       cyst, brachury, facial fold
       dermatitis, deafness, cleft
       palate (five percent), ana-
       sarca, entropion, collapsed
       trachea, swimmers, hydro-
       cephalus, hemivertebra,
       spina bifida, pulmonic ste-
       nosis, mitral valve defect,
       subaortic stenosis, tracheal
       hypoplasia, mast cell
       tumor, oligodendroglioma,
       distichiasis, extra incisor,
       factor VIII deficiency, kerra-
       titis sicca.

39. BULLMASTIFF
    A. Irregular cycles and ovula-
       tion, dry seasons, vaginal
       hyperplasia.
    B. Need help, cumbersome
       and low thyroid, ninety per-
       cent AI's.
    C. Five to eight.
    D. Sixteen to twenty-four.
    E. "Lazy" whelpers, need
       help, frequent cesareans,
       often lack milk.
    F. Remove rear or all.

I. Yellow eyes, no mask. Slight underbite normal. Short or screw tails.

J. Bad temperament, cleft palates, retinal atrophy—progressive, primary glaucoma, vaginal hyperplasia, large percentage hip dysplasia, gastric torsion, cervical vertebral instability, extra incisor, ununited anchoneal process.

40. CAIRN TERRIER
A. May have short seasons or outside ties due to hypothyroidism. Otherwise, OK.
B. Normal.
C. Three to five.
D. Five.
E. Free whelpers, good mothers.
F. Remove all.
G. Do not dock!!
J. Cryptorchidism, globoid cell leukodystrophy, factor VIII deficiency, factor IX deficiency, cerebellar hypoplasia, primary glaucoma, patellar luxation, hypothyroidism, cystinuria, craniomandibular osteopathy, recurrent tetany, von Willebrand's disease, lens luxation, retinal atrophy—generalized progressive.

41. CANAAN DOG
A. Normal.
B. Normal.
C. Four to five (three to nine).
D. Twelve.
E. Free whelpers; good, protective mothers.
F. Removal optional.
J. Epilepsy, retinal atrophy—progressive, hip dysplasia.

42. CARDIGAN WELSH CORGI
A. Normal.
B. Normal.
C. Five to eight.
D. Nine to twelve.
E. Some tendency for dystocia.
F. Remove rear, if present.
G. Do not dock!!
I. Mismarks, curly tails.
J. Corneal dermoid cyst, radius curvus, cleft palates, retinal atrophy—generalized progressive, glaucoma—primary, cystinuria, intervertebral disc disease, von Willebrand's disease, lens luxation, cutaneous asthenia, retinal dysplasia.

43. CASTRO LABOREIRO
A. As late as two years, not receptive first heat (sometimes never). If receptive—often pseudo-pregnancy. Irregular seasons.
B. Low libido.
C. Eight.
D Seventeen to thirty-one.
I. Live among sheep and even nurse from them.

44. CATAHOULA LEOPARD DOG
A. Normal.
B. Normal.
C. Eight to nine.
D. Large.
E. Good whelpers; have them by themselves.
G. Some born tailless.
J. None reported.

45. CAVALIER KING CHARLES SPANIEL
A. Normal.
B. Normal.

45. CAVALIER KING CHARLES
    SPANIEL (*cont.*)
  C. Four to five.
  D. Five to eight.
  E. Easy whelpers, good
     mothers.
  F. Remove all.
  G. If docked, leave two thirds
     to three fourths; must be
     white on end, so may not
     be able to dock at all.
  J. Underbites, cryptorchidism,
     fly biting syndrome, corneal
     dystrophy, patellar luxa-
     tion, diabetes mellitus—
     adult onset.

46. CHESAPEAKE BAY
    RETRIEVER
  A. Usually normal, some infer-
     tility, irregular seasons,
     hard to settle.
  B. Usually normal, some
     sterility.
  C. Eight to ten.
  D. Twelve to sixteen.
  E. Usually free whelpers,
     some inertias and dysto-
     cias, good mothers.
  F. Remove all.
  I. Soft or open coats.
  J. Retinal atrophy—central
     progressive, entropion, hip
     dysplasia, azospermia, von
     Willebrand's disease.

47. CHIHUAHUA
  A. Too small: frequent outside
     ties or AI's.
  B. Normal and eager. Accus-
     tom them to being handled.
  C. Two to five.
  D. Three to five, as small as
     two ounces survive.
  E. Small litters, inertia and
     sections frequent in some
     lines.

F. Remove all.
I. Open fontanel common (OK
   by Standard).
J. Retained baby teeth, bad
   bites, hypoglycemia—juvenile, missing canines, patellar luxation, cleft palates,
   kerratitis sicca, factor VIII
   deficiency, pulmonic stenosis, mitral valve defect,
   glaucoma, collapsed trachea, entropion, hydrocephalus, atlanto—axial
   subluxation, shoulder dislocation, foramen magnum
   enlargement, iris atrophy,
   spina bifida, lens luxation.

48. CHINESE CRESTED
  A. Normal.
  B. Normal.
  C. Three to four.
  D. Two to four.
  E. Easy whelpers, good
     mothers.
  F. Since "wash face" with
     paws, often removed.
  I. "Powder puff" coat.
  J. Bad underbites, allergy to
     lanolin (wool), 104° *normal*
     body temperature.

49. CHOW CHOW
  A. Often cycle more than
     twice a year. Hard to time
     ovulation, hard to settle.
  B. Lack of interest, low libido.
  C. Four to six.
  D. Ten to twenty.
  E. Hard to diagnose preg-
     nancy, cesareans common
     in very large or small litters.
  I. Short tails, poor pigmenta-
     tion, non-black tongue.
  J. Bad bites, elongated soft
     palate, distichiasis, congen-
     ital myotonia, entropion,

patellar luxation, hip dysplasia (forty percent), elbow dysplasia, poor temperament, hypothyroidism, cerebellar hypoplasia, sensitivity to anesthesia.

50. CLUMBER SPANIEL
A. Puberty at two years, irregular cycles.
B. Heavy males with low libido, AI's common.
C. Four to six.
D. Twelve to sixteen.
E. Some sections due to secondary inertia, hard conditioning may help with delivery. Overzealous mothers may mutilate newly docked tails.
F. Remove all.
G. Docked at taper—leave one third.
J. Underbite, wry mouth, missing teeth, ectropion, entropion, hip dysplasia, intervertebral disc disease.

51. COCKER SPANIEL
A. Normal.
B. Normal. May have shorter legs than female—use elevation.
C. Four to six.
D. Six to eight.
E. Free whelpers, good mothers.
F. Remove all.
G. Docked at taper—leave one third.
J. Bad bites, anury, umbilical hernia, cherry eye, ectropion, distichiasis, seborrhea, corneal dermoid cyst, skin and ear problems, cataract—juvenile, retinal atrophy—generalized progressive, hip dysplasia, ununited anchoneal process, bad temperaments, pseudohermaphrodites, inguinal hernia, reverse rear legs, factor X deficiency, anasarca, eosinophilic colitis, urolithiasis, foramen magnum enlargement, cleft lip and palate, cranioschisis, ectodermal defect, hydrocephalus, persistent right aortic arch, patent ductus arteriosus, cataract—with microphthalmia, factor IX deficiency, glaucoma—primary, autoimmune hemolytic anemia, entropion, luxated patellas, kerratitis sicca, intervertebral disc disease, achondroplasia, renal cortical hypoplasia, aseptic necrosis of femoral head, hypothyroidism, epilepsy, spondylosis deformans, lymphosarcoma, retinal dysplasia.

52. COLLIE (ROUGH AND SMOOTH)
A. Easy breeders, although strictures and polyps are frequent.
B. Normal.
C. Six to ten.
D. Twelve.
E. Easy whelpers, pups often have low "survival drive."
F. Remove rear if present; front optional.
H. Tape or glue, if not tipping properly by twelve weeks.
I. Wall eye, mismarks.
J. Overbite, underbite, nasal solar dermatitis, umbilical hernia, gingival hyperplasia, distichiasis, dwarfism,

52. COLLIE (ROUGH AND SMOOTH) (*cont.*)
ectasia, retinal atrophy—generalized progressive, factor VIII deficiency, deafness, corneal dystrophy, cleft palates, choroidal hypoplasia, optic nerve hypoplasia, cyclic neutropenia, patent ductus arteriosus, fibrinogen deficiency, tarsal subluxation, pseudohermaphrodites, osteogenesis imperfecta, retinal atrophy—central progressive.

53. COTON DE TULEAR
A. Normal.
B. Normal.
C. Five to eight.
D. Small.
E. Normal, free whelpers.
J. None.

54. CURLY-COATED RETRIEVER
A. Lots of misses, always check thyroid.
B. Generally normal, but some sterility.
C. Six to nine.
D. Eight to fourteen.
E. Free whelpers, pyometras common.
F. Remove all.
I. Light eyes and/or nose, especially in liver color, bald spots, missing hair, coat not curly or only curly on part of body.
J. Entropion (corrects with age), hyperadrenocorticism, hypothyroidism, juvenile osteoparesis, von Willebrand's disease, bilateral alopecia.

55. DACHSHUND (ALL VARIETIES)
A. May have to muzzle, many false pregnancies, retire at five years.
B. Keep males apart. Because of shape, may need assistance with breeding.
C. Two to four (mini), five (standard).
D. Four to six (mini), eight to ten (standard).
E. Usually free whelpers, but inertia frequent. Cesareans more frequent in minis. Good mothers.
F. Remove rear, if present.
I. Wall eye, improper coat texture (especially wires), screw or kink tail.
J. Bad bites, umbilical hernia, distichiasis, trichiasis, corneal dermoid cyst, atopic dermatitis, swimmers, achalasia, ectasia, microphthalmia, pannus—atypical, intervertebral disc disease, hemi vertebra (minis), cataracts, kerratitis sicca, diabetes mellitus—adult onset, cystinuria, renal cortical hypoplasia, deafness, cleft lip and palate, epilepsy, hypothyroidism, spondylosis deformans, von Willebrand's disease, patellar luxation, osteopetrosis, hyperadrenocorticism, retinal atrophy—generalized progressive, ununited anchoneal process, lens luxation.

56. DALMATIAN
A. Normal.
B. Normal.

C. Eight to ten (thirteen not unusual).
D. Eleven to fifteen.
E. Normal.
F. Remove all.
I. Unpigmented eye rims, patches (colored spots present at birth), tri or lemon spots.
J. Atopic dermatitis, deafness, uric acid stones, diabetes mellitus—adult onset, spina bifida, globoid cell leukodystrophy.

57. DANDIE DINMONT TERRIER
A. Fairly normal, some small tracts.
B. Late maturity, mostly normal, some AI's.
C. Four to six.
D. Eight to ten.
E. Hard to diagnose pregnancy, weight gain by thirty-five days is best.
F. Remove all.
J. Bad bites, intervertebral disc disease, hip dysplasia, patellar luxation, dislocated shoulder, elbow joint deformity.

58. DOBERMAN PINSCHER
A. Normal.
B. Normal, some reluctant breeders—train early.
C. Eight.
D. Sixteen.
E. Easy whelpers, although small litters can create problems. Some hysterical mothers.
F. Remove all.
G. Docked not quite to end of tan mark—or leave one half inch at two to three days.

H. Cropped with moderate length, smooth base and graceful curve, best at six to eight weeks.
J. Color mutant alopecia, bad bites, flank sucking, vestibular disorder, cervical vertebral instability, craniomandibular osteopathy, renal cortical hypoplasia, von Willebrand's disease, hypothyroidism, narcolepsy, demodectic mange, spondylolisthesis, polyostotic fibrous dysplasia, diabetes mellitus—juvenile onset.

59. ENGLISH COCKER SPANIEL
A. Normal.
B. Normal.
C. Five.
D. Eight to ten.
E. Easy whelpers.
F. Remove all.
G. Docked, leave one third.
J. Swimmers, retained baby teeth, cryptorchidism, pseudohermaphrodites, vestibular disorder, retinal atrophy—generalized progressive, factor VIII deficiency, neuromal ceroid lipofucinosis, von Willebrand's disease, prothrombin deficiency.

60. ENGLISH FOXHOUND
A. Normal.
B. No interest—would rather go hunting, especially older pack hounds.
C. Eight.
D. Sixteen to twenty.
E. Slow, free whelpers, not too interested in pups. Place pups in homes for

60. ENGLISH FOXHOUND
(*cont.*)
one year to develop
personality.
F. Remove all.
H. "Rounded" (one quarter of
ear removed) at about one
year (after they become
full-fledged members of
hunting pack).
I. (Not registered until mem-
ber of working pack.)
J. Very few, all working
hounds. Cancers in older
dogs.

61. ENGLISH SETTER
A. Long, excessive estrus flow,
irregular ovulation, poor
fertility.
B. Low libido in some strains.
C. Six to ten (or more).
D. Sixteen.
E. Inertia from eclampsia frequent—after calcium may
whelp rest of litter. Too
much milk, caked breasts
common even with large
litters.
F. Remove all.
J. Vaginitis, ectropion, umbilical hernia, craniomandibular osteopathy, deafness
(seventy-five percent carry
recessive), neuromal ceroid
lipofucinosis, factor VIII deficiency, retinal atrophy—
central progressive, retinal
atrophy—generalized
progressive.

62. ENGLISH SPRINGER
SPANIEL
A. Normal.
B. Normal.
C. Seven to eight.
D. Nine to fourteen.

E. Easy whelpers, but watch
they don't get too fat.
F. Remove all.
G. Docked, leave one third of
tail.
J. Underbites, ectropion, seborrhea, ear problems, obesity, retinal atrophy—central progressive, hip
dysplasia, entropion, glaucoma, factor XI deficiency,
cutaneous asthenia, von
Willebrand's disease, achalasia, subaortic stenosis,
distichiasis, retinal dysplasia, retinal atrophy—generalized progressive.

63. ENGLISH TOY SPANIEL
A. Late onset of puberty for
toy (twelve to fourteen
months).
B. Slow to mature, normal
breeders.
C. Two to six.
D. Four to six.
E. Usually normal, some slow,
some cesareans due to
large pups.
F. Remove all.
G. Docked, leave one and one
half inches at four to five days.
I. Any white on black/tan or
ruby colors.
J. Hanging tongue, umbilical
hernias, open fontanel, lux-
ating patellas, diabetes
mellitus.

64. FIELD SPANIEL
A. Irregular seasons, often two
years apart; pyometras.
B. Normal.
C. Six.
D. Sixteen.
E. Pyometras common, free
whelpers.
F. Remove all.

G. Docked, leave two fifths of tail.

I. Lack of coat (especially livers).

J. Hypothyroidism, hip dysplasia, pyometritis.

65. FINNISH SPITZ
A. Normal.
B. Normal.
C. Three to four.
D. Six to eight.
E. Free whelpers, good mothers.
I. White patch on chest or toes.
J. Cataracts.

66. FLAT-COATED RETRIEVER
A. Normal.
B. Normal.
C. Three to four.
D. Six to eight.
E. Free whelpers, good moms.
F. Removal optional.
I. Yellows, faded pigment in livers.
J. Hypothyroidism, hip dysplasia, retinal atrophy—progressive, patellar luxation.

67. FOX TERRIER (WIRE AND SMOOTH)
A. Normal.
B. Normal.
C. Eight.
D. Eleven to thirteen.
E. Fairly normal, a few inertias.
F. Remove all.
G. Docked, leave a generous two-thirds (even with top of head).
H. Glue at seven to eight weeks, if not tipping properly.
I. Gay tails.
J. Bad bites, distichiasis, lens luxation, achalasia, deafness, cataracts—juvenile, ataxia, dislocated shoulder, aseptic necrosis of femoral head, oligodontia, pulmonic stenosis, subaortic stenosis, persistent right aortic arch, cleft palate, goiter, cervical vertebral instability, tetralogy of Fallot, hypospadia.

68. FRENCH BULLDOG
A. Small tracts, secure female or AI.
B. Most AI's due to body shape.
C. Four to five.
D. Six to eight.
E. Small pelvis, large pup heads, inertias—result in most cesareans.
J. Elongated soft palate, upper respiratory problems, clefts of lip and palate, hemivertebra, brachury, factor VIII deficiency, factor IX deficiency, genito-urinary carcinomas, lens luxation, intervertebral disc disease, patellar luxation, spondylosis deformans, ataxia, ununited anchoneal process, retinal atrophy—progressive.

69. GERMAN SHEPHERD DOG
A. Normal, some strictures. Some four-month cycles.
B. Most normal, a few lazy breeders.
C. Eight to ten.
D. Twelve to twenty.
E. Generally free whelpers and good mothers. Very large pups may require assistance.
F. Remove rear if present; front optional.

69. GERMAN SHEPHERD DOG
(*cont.*)
H. Tape, if not standing by twelve weeks.
I. Long coats; whites, blues and livers (disqualifying colors), heavy ear leather.
J. Cryptorchidism, corneal dermoid cyst, perianal fistula, nictitating membrane eversion, enostosis, achalasia, persistent right aortic arch, hip dysplasia, ununited anchoneal process, pannus, patent ductus arteriosus, epilepsy, poor temperaments, malabsorption syndrome, diabetes mellitus—juvenile onset, calcium gout, eosinophilic colitis, spondylosis deformans, intervertebral disc disease, osteochondritis dessicans, cataract—bilateral, ectasia, subaortic stenosis, cystinuria, factor VIII deficiency, von Willebrand's disease, renal cortical hypoplasia, pituitary dwarfism, cleft lip and palate, degenerative myelopathy, chronic pancreatitis, distichiasis, cerebellar hypoplasia, missing teeth, toxic gut syndrome, retinal atrophy—generalized progressive.

70. GERMAN SHORTHAIR POINTER
A. May cycle more than twice a year, ovulation time varies. Many false pregnancies.
B. Shy breeders in some lines.
C. Ten.
D. Nine to fifteen.

E. Very few may have eclampsia during delivery, good mothers, heavy milkers.
F. Remove all.
G. Docked, leave a generous two fifth of tail.
J. Underbites, nictitating membrane eversion, pannus, high strung nervous temperaments, gastric torsion, atresia ani, hip dysplasia, entropion, lymphedema, von Willebrand's disease, thrombopathia, subaortic stenosis, epilepsy, osteochondritis dessicans, gangliosidosis.

71. GERMAN WIREHAIR POINTER
A. Normal.
B. Normal.
C. Ten.
D. Nine to fifteen.
E. Free whelpers, good mothers.
F. Remove all.
G. Docked, leave just under half of tail.
I. Wispy soft coats, long woolly coats, smooth coats.
J. Bad bites, hip dysplasia.

72. GIANT SCHNAUZER
A. Don't settle well if shipped.
B. Normal, but late to mature.
C. Seven to nine.
D. Six to sixteen.
E. Frequent secondary inertia, very protective of pups.
F. Remove all.
G. Docked, second or third vertebra.
H. Cropped, similar to Dobe.
J. Bad bites, missing teeth, cowhocks, cryptorchidism, hip dysplasia, poor temper-

aments, osteochondritis dessicans, pulmonic stenosis, retinal atrophy—progressive.

73. GOLDEN RETRIEVER
A. Some long cyclers, otherwise normal.
B. Good, but not very eager.
C. Six to eight.
D. Sixteen to twenty-four.
E. Free whelpers, good mothers.
F. Remove all.
I. Mismarks.
J. Cryptorchidism, missing teeth, bad bites, wry mouths, ectropion, swimmers, immune deficiency, hip dysplasia, entropion, cleft palate, retinal atrophy—central progressive, von Willebrand's disease, hypothyroidism, cataract—bilateral, cerebellar hypoplasia, retinal atrophy—generalized progressive, cataract with microphthalmia, epilepsy, diabetes mellitus—juvenile onset.

74. GORDON SETTER
A. Ovulation variation, otherwise normal.
B. Normal.
C. Eight to twelve.
D. Twelve to sixteen.
E. Easy whelpers, good mothers.
F. Removal optional.
I. Red color, too much white, crooked tails.
J. Cerebellar cortical abiotrophy, hip dysplasia, hypothyroidism, shyness, retinal atrophy—generalized progressive, retinal dysplasia.

75. GREAT DANE
A. Many false pregnancies, otherwise normal.
B. Normal and eager. Height difference in large males—breed downhill.
C. Nine.
D. Twenty-four.
E. Usually free whelpers, sometimes large litters with large pups bring secondary inertia and section.
F. Removal optional.
H. Cropped, long and graceful with clean base, seven to nine weeks best.
I. Mismarks, too much white (on all colors), illegal colors, wall eye.
J. Cryptorchidism, bad bites, short life, calluses, nictitating membrane eversion, ectropion, flat feet, fear biters and other temperament problems, cervical vertebral instability, hip dysplasia, ununited anchoneal process, gastric torsion, osteochondritis dessicans, Stockard's paralysis, calcium gout, mitral valve defect, cystinuria, degenerative myelopathy, cerebellar hypoplasia, hypertrophic osteodystrophy, spondylosis deformans, entropion, spondylolisthesis, osteogenic sarcoma, von Willebrand's disease.

76. GREAT PYRENEES
A. Cycles regular, but ovulation erratic.
B. May need assistance.
C. Six to seven.
D. Sixteen.

76. GREAT PYRENEES (*cont.*)
E. Usually free whelpers but over three-hour delay between pups may require interference. Good mothers, but may roll on pups during first few days.
F. Double rear dewclaws required; leave all.
I. Normal body temp low, blue eyes.
J. Bad bites, missing dewclaws, slow metabolism—caution with anesthesia, hip dysplasia, entropion, patellar luxation, cataracts—juvenile, spondylosis deformans, metritis, ununited anchoneal process, factor XI deficiency.

77. GREATER SWISS MOUNTAIN DOG
A. Normal.
B. Normal.
C. Eight to nine.
D. Sixteen.
E. Free whelpers, good mothers.
F. Remove all.
I. Liver tri can occur.
J. Hip dysplasia, very high incidence of gastric torsion.

78. GREYHOUND
A. Puberty at two years or more, cycle nine months to one year, may not stand, AI's common.
B. Slow to mature, low libido. Taller than female, AI's common.
C. Seven to ten (fifteen not unknown).
D. Sixteen to thirty.
E. Dystocias frequent due to long slow delivery of many large pups. Scream during delivery, often lots of blood. Carry high, x-ray to be sure done. Fetal death rate high. Good mothers.
F. Remove all.
I. Light eyes.
J. Cryptorchidism, gastric torsion, elbow bursitis, achalasia, factor VIII deficiency, short spine, hypersensitivity to anesthesia, spina bifida, lens luxation, calcium gout, persistent right aortic arch, retinal atrophy—generalized progressive.

79. HARRIER
A. Normal.
B. Normal.
C. Eight to ten.
D. Eight to ten.
E. Free whelpers.
F. Dewclaws usually removed for show, optional for field work.
J. Malocclusion.

80. HAVANESE
A. Normal.
B. Aggressive breeders, but don't fight among themselves.
C. Four to nine.
D. Six.
E. Free whelpers, good moms.
F. Rear removed, if present.
I. Lack of pigment.
J. Bad mouths.

81. IBIZAN HOUNDS
A. Puberty two years or more, cycle ten months to one year. Extreme false pregnancies.
B. Normal.
C. Six to twelve.
D. Fourteen.

E. Easy whelpers, good mothers.
F. Remove all.
J. Cryptorchidism, umbilical hernias, hypersensitivity to anesthetics and insecticides.

82. IRISH SETTER
A. Late puberty, erratic cycles with some false seasons. Many false pregnancies.
B. Normal.
C. Eight to ten.
D. Sixteen.
E. Secondary inertia common. Hyperactive first two to three days; watch closely—may step on pup. Eclampsia frequent.
F. Remove all, especially field stock.
I. Kink and stub tails.
J. Underbites, overbites, ectropion, enostosis, osteochondritis dessicans, hypertrophic osteodystrophy, hip dysplasia, carpal subluxation, persistent right aortic arch, perianal fistula, hypothyroidism, entropion, metritis, gastric torsion, retinal atrophy—generalized progressive, factor VIII deficiency, cervical vertebral instability, quadriplegia with ambliopia, generalized myopathy, epilepsy, von Willebrand's disease, retinal atrophy—central progressive.

83. IRISH TERRIER
A. Normal.
B. Normal.
C. Four to eight.
D. Eight.

E. Easy whelpers, very independent and protective, good mothers.
F. Remove all.
G. Docked, leave two-thirds to three-quarters of tail (even with top of head).
H. If not folding properly, start setting at twelve weeks through one year.
I. Soft coats.
J. Cystinuria, bad teeth.

84. IRISH WATER SPANIEL
A. Ovulation variation, may not stand, some misses.
B. Mostly normal, a few infertile or sterile males.
C. Eight to ten.
D. Twelve to sixteen.
E. Free whelpers, tend to "sling" pups out, good mothers.
F. Remove all.
I. Coat problems (lack of curl, alopecia), variation in size, kink in tail.
J. Hip dysplasia, hypothyroidism, shyness (especially at puberty).

85. IRISH WOLFHOUND
A. Puberty at eighteen to twenty-four months, cycle six to nine months.
B. Some low libido. If willing, dignified and easy to handle.
C. Five to six.
D. Twenty to twenty-four.
E. Long deliveries, secondary inertia or section often halfway through. May lay on pups; watch carefully first week.
F. Remove all.
J. Elbow hygroma, gastric tor-

85. IRISH WOLFHOUND (*cont.*)
sion, hip dysplasia, entropion, ununited anchoneal
process, calcium gout,
osteosarcoma.

86. ITALIAN GREYHOUND
A. Normal, but puberty may
be eighteen to twenty-four
months.
B. Normal, testes late to
descend.
C. Three to five.
D. Six to nine.
E. Natural whelpers, a few
inertias. They'll mother orphan pups easily.
F. Remove all.
J. Retained baby teeth,
crooked teeth, receding
gums with tooth loss, achalasia, persistent right aortic arch, epilepsy, hypersensitivity to barbiturates
and insecticides, patellar
luxation.

87. JACK RUSSELL TERRIER
A. Normal.
B. Normal.
C. Four to six.
D. Four to eight.
E. Free whelpers, good mothers.
F. Remove all.
G. Docked, leave half.
I. Prick ears.
J. Poor temperament, myas-
thenia gravis, ataxia, lens
luxation, patellar luxation,
aseptic necrosis of femoral
head.

88. JAPANESE SPANIEL
(CHIN)
A. Normal.
B. Normal libido, need assis-
tance for aim and height
difference.

C. Three to five.
D. Three to four.
E. Pups have large heads, but
usually no problems. Help
with cords, good mothers.
F. Remove rear, front
optional.
J. Cryptorchidism, patellar
luxation, wry mouths.

89. KEESHOND
A. Often ovulate late in cycle.
B. Normal.
C. Five to seven.
D. Eight to twelve.
E. Seventy days not unknown,
free whelpers, good
mothers.
F. Remove all.
J. Hip dysplasia, epilepsy, hypothyroidism, renal cortical
hypoplasia, tetralogy of Fallot, metritis, mitral valve
defect, diabetes mellitus—
juvenile onset, retinal atrophy—generalized
progressive.

90. KERRY BLUE TERRIER
A. May ovulate early, small
immature tracts, hard to
settle.
B. Need lots of "get ac-
quainted" time, poor aim.
C. Five.
D. Eight to twelve.
E. Often whelp early, dysto-
cias not unknown. Some do
not want to stay and care
for pups, especially spoiled
house pets.
F. Remove all.
G. Dock, leave two-thirds
H. Glued to proper fold posi-
tion at eight weeks.
I. No fading (stay black).
J. Cerebellar cortical abiotro-

phy, entropion, kerratitis sicca, Factor XI deficiency.

91. KOMONDOR
A. Sometimes late puberty, cycle eight months. Ovulate late in heat (fourteen to sixteen days).
B. Low libido, more interested in guard duty. Problems with heavy coats. Sometimes no conception, even when breeding accomplished.
C. Five to eight.
D. Sixteen.
E. Free whelpers, good mothers. Have formula ready, often late to come into milk. Many fading pups, especially when too warm.
F. Remove all.
I. Faded pigment, light eyes.
J. Underbites, misaligned incisors, hip dysplasia, shy temperaments, gastric torsion.

92. KUVASZ
A. Normal.
B. Normal.
C. Seven to eight.
D. Sixteen to twenty-four.
E. Free whelpers, good mothers.
F. Remove rear, if present.
I. Yellow in coat, blue eyes, "satin" coats (too fine, long and open).
J. Hip dysplasia, osteochondritis dessicans, temperament problems.

93. KYI-LEO
A. Normal, may cycle nine months. Some spoiled brats.
B. Can be a bit shy if not trained properly.
C. Three to four.
D. Four to seven.
E. Free whelpers, good mothers.
J. Patellar luxation, flea allergy.

94. LABRADOR RETRIEVER
A. May not stand well, usually normal.
B. Normal.
C. Seven to eight.
D. Twelve to sixteen.
E. Free whelpers, good mothers.
F. Remove all.
I. Mismarks or improper colors, lack of pigment.
J. Cryptorchidism, bad bites and missing teeth, cataract—bilateral, retinal dysplasia, retinal atrophy—central progressive, entropion, cystinuria, retinal atrophy—generalized progressive, epilepsy, mastocytoma, lens luxation, chondrodysplasia, diabetes mellitus—juvenile onset, distichiasis, achalasia, calcium gout, factor VIII deficiency, carpal subluxation, hip dysplasia, ununited anchoneal process, craniomandibular osteopathy, osteochondritis dessicans, hypertrophic osteodystrophy, hypothyroidism, prolapsed rectum, deficiency of type II muscle fibers, von Willebrand's disease, Factor IX deficiency.

95. LAKELAND TERRIER
A. Some lines late puberty at twenty to twenty-four

95. LAKELAND TERRIER
    (*cont.*)
    months, twelve- to fifteen-
    month intervals common in
    cold kennels.
    B. Normal, some sterile dogs.
    C. Four to five.
    D. Eight.
    E. Free whelpers, if not over-
       weight, good mothers.
    F. Remove all.
    G. Docked, to level with top of
       head.
    I. Livers with faded pigment.
    J. Underbites, cryptorchidism,
       distichiasis, ununited an-
       choneal process, lens luxa-
       tion, aseptic necrosis of
       femoral head, von Wille-
       brand's disease.

96. LEONBERGER
    A. Normal, some four-month
       cyclers.
    B. Normal.
    C. Eight.
    D. Sixteen.
    E. Free whelpers, good
       mothers.
    F. Remove rear dewclaws.
    J. None reported.

97. LHASA APSO
    A Normal.
    B. Normal.
    C. Three to five.
    D. Five to seven.
    E. Generally free whelpers,
       but large pup heads and
       poor muscle tone may
       cause problems. Normal
       underbite, can't cut cord
       properly.
    F. Remove all.
    J. Umbilical hernia, disti-
       chiasis, inguinal hernia, en-
       tropion, patellar luxation,

retinal atrophy—progres-
sive, renal cortical hypoplasia, ADH absence, hip
dysplasia, lissencephaly, intervertebral disc disease,
von Willebrand's disease.

98. LITTLE LION DOG
    (LOWCHEN)
    A. Normal, some cycle just
       once a year.
    B. Normal.
    C. Three to four.
    D. Five to seven.
    E. Free whelpers, good
       mothers.
    F. Remove all.
    J. Underbites, wry mouths,
       patellar luxation, aseptic
       necrosis of femoral head.

99. MALTESE
    A. Very short seasons, false
       pregnancies frequent.
    B. Normal, but very tiny male
       may require assistance.
    C. Two to four.
    D. Three to six.
    E. Show bitches in six-pound
       range often too small and
       require cesarean. Occa-
       sional eclampsia. Some in-
       different mothers.
    F. Remove all.
    I. Lemon color on side coat.
    J. Retained puppy teeth, mis-
       aligned teeth, hypoglyce-
       mia—juvenile, cryptorchid-
       ism, hydrocephalus, open
       fontanel, clefts of lip and
       palate, entropion, patellar
       luxation, deafness.

100. MANCHESTER TERRIER
     (STANDARD AND TOY)
     A. One to one and one-half
        years, puberty normal.

B. Normal.

C. Three (Toy), five to six (Standard).

D. Five to six.

E. Free whelpers.

F. Generally remove all.

H. Standard: cropped moderately long and smooth. Toy: do not crop; tape if not up by six months.

I. Incorrect size (both).

J. Retained puppy teeth, umbilical hernias, von Willebrand's disease, luxated lens, cleft palate, epilepsy, cutaneous asthenia, aseptic necrosis of femoral head, hydrocephalus.

101. MAREMMA SHEEPDOG
A.–D. Similar to the Castro Laboreiro.

102. MASTIFF
A. Irregular seasons and ovulation, many resorptions and false pregnancies, vaginal hyperplasia and prolapse.

B. Sometimes low sperm count and low libido, may be due to hypothyroidism.

C. Five (can be up to fourteen).

D. Sixteen to twenty-four.

E. Secondary inertia after one or two pups, vaginal hyperplasia and prolapse also frequent.

I. Screw tails, obesity.

J. Ectropion, hypothyroidism, shy temperaments, vaginal hyperplasia, hip dysplasia.

103. MEXICAN HAIRLESS AND XOLOITZCUINTLI
A. Normal, but frequent misses.

B. Normal.

C. Three.

D. Four.

E. Free whelpers, good mothers.

I. "Coateds" culled, drop ears, bad fronts.

J. Covered ear canal.

104. MINIATURE BULL TERRIER
A. Normal.

B. Normal.

C. Three to four.

D. Six.

E. Usually free whelpers, good moms. Some eclampsia.

J. Bred down from standard size, same problems.

105. MINIATURE PINSCHER
A. Normal, a few very dominant bitches.

B. Normal and eager.

C. One to six.

D. Four to six.

E. If kept muscular and trim, hardy free whelpers.

F. Remove all.

G. Docked short, not quite to end of tan or just cover anal triangle.

H. Cropped, moderate length, narrow curved and graceful.

I. Oversized, lack of eye/nose pigment, white spots, "thumb" marks.

J. Retained baby teeth, cleft palates, inguinal hernias, aseptic necrosis of femoral head; shoulder dislocation, retinal atrophy—general progressive, kerratitis sicca.

106. MINIATURE POODLE
A. Puberty often fourteen months or more, normal breeders.

B. Normal, eager.

106. MINIATURE POODLE
(*cont.*)
C. Four to six.
D. Six to eight.
E. Free whelpers, good mothers.
F. Remove all.
G. Docked, leave over half of tail, remove just over one-third.
I. Particolors.
J. Bad bites, atopic dermatitis, distichiasis, epiphora, pseudohermaphrodites, cryptorchidism, missing teeth, achondroplasia, naso-lacrimal duct atresia, entropion, cataract—juvenile, retinal atrophy—general progressive, pannus atypical, hyperadrenocorticism, Freidreich's ataxia, kerratitis sicca, hydrocephalus, hip dysplasia, Lafora's disease, microphthalmia, collapsed trachea, dislocated shoulder, diabetes mellitus—juvenile onset, ectasia, cystinuria, ectodermal defect, atlanto-axial subluxation, hemeralopia, von Willebrand's disease, ectopic ureters, patent ductus arteriosus, deafness, epiphyseal dysplasia, intervertebral disc disease, epilepsy, aseptic necrosis of femoral head, patellar luxation, globoid cell leukodystrophy, gangliosidosis, cerebrospinal demyelinization.

107. MINIATURE SCHNAUZER
A. Ovulation variation, often late, many "spoiled brats."
B. Outside ties can be a problem.
C. Three to five.
D. Four to nine.

E. Lazy bitches, about fifteen percent require cesarean.
F. Remove all.
G. Docked, just short of tan mark.
H. Cropped, moderately short, curved, with no bell.
I. White spots, pure white, soft wispy coats, late eruptions of baby teeth at forty to fifty days.
J. Cryptorchidism, follicular dermatitis, pseudohermaphrodites, bad bites, Schnauzer comodome syndrome, cleft palates, cystitis and uroliths, sertoli cell tumor, sino-atrial syncope, achalasia, pulmonic stenosis, cataracts—juvenile, aseptic necrosis of femoral head, von Willebrand's disease, hypothyroidism, kerratitis sicca, atopic dermatitis, epilepsy, ectasia, Factor VII deficiency, microphthalmia.

108. NEOPOLITAN MASTIFF
A. Normal, but aggressive. Introduce to male early in season.
B. Normal.
C. Twelve.
D. Sixteen to twenty-four.
E. Free whelpers, good mothers.
F. Rears removed.
G. Dock, leave two-thirds.
H. Very short ear crop.
J. Ectropion, screw tails, cherry eye, hip dysplasia, down in pastern (or radius curvus).

109. NEWFOUNDLAND
A. Uncooperative, awkward. Irregular ovulation.

B. Awkward, need help. No ties—hold male up.

C. Six.

D. Twenty to twenty-four.

E. Long, slow whelpers, watch for last pup or two to be stillborn or retained, secondary inertia. *Not* protective, good mothers.

F. Remove rear, if present.

J. Underbites, nictitating membrane eversion, corneal dermoid cyst, hypothyroidism, umbilical hernias, gastric torsion, hip dysplasia, ununited anchoneal process, hemivertebra, subaortic stenosis, patent ductus arteriosus.

110. NORWEGIAN ELKHOUND

A. Normal.

B. May not mature until two to two and one-half years.

C. Five to seven.

D. Eight to ten.

E. Free whelpers, many squat to deliver, then lie down between pups.

F. Remove rear, if present.

J. Bad bites, sebaceous cysts, hip dysplasia, retinal atrophy—generalized progressive, renal cortical hypoplasia, osteogenesis imperfecta, entropion, cleft palates, chondrodysplasia.

111. NORWICH/NORFOLK TERRIER

A. Normal, if not spoiled.

B. May require assistance, due to short legs. Normal if take time to train.

C. Two to three.

D. Three to four.

E. May require assistance, usually free whelpers.

Some sections in smaller bitches with large pups.

F. Remove all.

G. Docked, just short of half, shorter than most Terriers.

I. Soft and long coats.

J. Bad mouths.

112. NOVA SCOTIA DUCK TOLLING RETRIEVER

A. Normal.

B. Normal.

C. Six to seven.

D. Twelve.

E. Free whelpers, good mothers.

F. Usually removed.

J. Hip dysplasia, retinal atrophy—progressive, immune deficiency.

113. OLD ENGLISH SHEEPDOG

A. Normal.

B. Normal.

C. Eight.

D. Ten to sixteen.

E. Free whelpers, good mothers.

F. Remove all.

G. Docked, as close to body as possible.

J. Bad bites, hip dysplasia, cataracts—juvenile, retinal dysplasia, cervical vertebral instability, entropion, diabetes mellitus—juvenile onset, deafness, Factor IX deficiency.

114. OTTER HOUND

A. Very small breed base, may have decreased fertility and irregular seasons.

B. If rarely used, may require AI.

C. Seven to eight.

D. Twenty.

E. Free whelpers, unless

114. OTTER HOUND (*cont.*)
older. Very attentive mothers for first two weeks.
   F. Removal optional.
   J. Bad bites (overbites often correct), cryptorchidism, hip dysplasia, thrombocytopathy, hypoprothrombinemia.

115. OWCZAREK NIZINNY
   A. Normal, eight-month cycles.
   B. Normal.
   C. Four to seven.
   D. Ten.
   E. Free whelpers, good mothers.
   G. Docked, short like Dobe.
   I. Faded nose, eye pigment.
   J. Underbites, hip dysplasia, entropion, patent ductus arteriosus.

116. OWCZAREK PODHALANSKI
   A. Late puberty, normal.
   B. Normal.
   C. Six to nine.
   D. Fourteen.
   E. Free whelpers, good mothers.
   F. Removal optional.
   G. Hip dysplasia.

117. PAPILLON
   A. Normal.
   B. Eager, but may need assistance if a lot smaller than female.
   C. Two to four.
   D. Four to five.
   E. Some free whelping lines. Primary inertia a problem, especially in single-pup litters. Eclampsia a problem.
   F. Remove all.
   I. Mismarks.

   J. Retained baby teeth, trichiasis, patellar luxation, inguinal hernia, entropion, von Willebrand's disease.

118. PEKINGESE
   A. Short estrus.
   B. Require assistance due to long coat and body shape.
   C. Three to five.
   D. Four to six.
   E. Delivery difficult, often sections. Need help to sever cord and clean pups. Good mothers.
   J. Umbilical hernia, distichiasis, stenotic nares and elongated soft palate, inguinal hernia, clefts of lip and palate, intervertebral disc disease, uroliths, lacrimal duct atresia, cataract—juvenile, microphthalmia, pannus—atypical, retinal atrophy—progressive, atlanto-axial subluxation, aseptic necrosis of the femoral head, patellar luxation, trichiasis, hydrocephalus.

119. PEMBROKE WELSH CORGI
   A. Normal.
   B. Normal.
   C. Six to seven.
   D. Ten.
   E. Mostly free whelpers, some tendency to dystocia. Often slow to begin tending to newborns.
   F. Remove all.
   G. If not born tailless, dock as close to body as possible.
   H. Tape, if not standing by twelve weeks.
   I. "Blues," all white, "fluffies."
   J. Bad bites, corneal dermoid

cyst, poor temperament, intervertebral disc disease, epilepsy, cystinuria, hip dysplasia, lens luxation, retinal atrophy—general progressive, "swimmers," cutaneous asthenia, von Willebrand's disease (thirty percent), retinal dysplasia.

120. PERUVIAN INCA ORCHID
   A. Late puberty, normal.
   B. Normal.
   C. Six.
   D. Ten to twelve.
   E. Free whelpers, good mothers.
   F. Removal optional.
   J. Umbilical hernias, missing teeth (associated with hairlessness, cross with coated to retain teeth).

121. PETIT BASSET GRIFFON VENDEEN
   A. Normal.
   B. Normal, train young.
   C. Nine to ten.
   D. Fourteen to sixteen.
   E. Free whelpers, good mothers—will continue training their pups and working with them, even when older.
   I. Ear injuries in the hunting packs.
   J. Limited gene pool, none reported; mostly working dogs.

122. PHARAOH HOUND
   A. Late puberty and ovulation, normal.
   B. Normal.
   C. Two to twelve.
   D. Depends on litter size.
   E. Free whelpers, *great* mothers.

F. Remove all.
I. Too much white, too large or small.
J. Hardy—none yet!

123. PIT BULL TERRIER
   A. Normal, some aggressive bitches.
   B. Normal.
   C. Six to nine.
   D. Eight to twelve.
   E. Free whelpers, good mothers.
   H. Optional short ear crop.
   I. Variation in size and type.
   J. Atopic dermatitis.

124. POINTER
   A. Normal.
   B. Slow to mature, otherwise normal.
   C. Six to fourteen.
   D. Ten to eighteen.
   E. Easy whelpers, sometimes a little early, good mothers.
   F. Remove all.
   J. Underbites, timid, umbilical hernia, entropion, cataract—bilateral, hip dysplasia, neurotropic osteopathy, bithoracic ectomelia, calcium gout, enostosis, ununited anchoneal process retinal atrophy—generalized progressive, retinal atrophy—central progressive.

125. POMERANIAN
   A. Normal, some dry heats.
   B. Normal.
   C. Two.
   D. Three to five.
   E. Some slow whelpers, live pups may follow two hours of mild but continuous contractions. Many free whelpers, good mothers.

125. POMERANIAN (*cont.*)
F. Remove all.
J. Cryptorchidism, hypoglycemia—juvenile, epiphora,
retained baby teeth, patellar luxation, open fontanel,
hydrocephalus, tracheal col-
lapse, patent ductus arteriosus, dislocated shoulder, atlanto-axial subluxation,
retinal atrophy—progres-
sive, naso-lacrimal duct
atresia, entropion,
distichiasis.

126. PORTUGUESE WATER
DOG
A. Normal.
B. Normal.
C. Eight.
D. Sixteen.
E. Free whelpers, may be a
bit nervous. Leave them be
and don't fuss.
I. Open coats.
J. Hip dysplasia.

127. PUG
A. Late puberty for Toy, nine
to twelve months.
B. Early puberty. Can become
exhausted before consum-
mated, if fat, during hot
weather.
C. Four to six.
D. Four to nine.
E. Some free whelping strains,
others a lot of inertia and
sections. Problems if overweight. Always need help
with cord and sac. Pups
slow to get going, often get
upper respiratory disease.
F. Remove all.
J. Elongated soft palate, pseudohermaphrodites, entro-
pion, aseptic necrosis of
femoral head, trichiasis,
pannus atypical.

128. PULI
A. Normal.
B. Normal.
C. Five to seven.
D. Seven to nine.
E. Free whelpers, good
mothers.
F. Remove all.
I. Particolors.
J. Underbites, missing teeth,
hip dysplasia.

129. RAT TERRIER
A. Normal.
B. Normal.
C. Five to seven.
D. Six.
E. Free whelpers, good
mothers.
G. Docked short.
J. Patellar luxation, lens
luxation.

130. RHODESIAN RIDGEBACK
A. Normal.
B. Normal.
C. Eight to ten.
D. Sixteen.
E. Free whelpers, good
mothers.
F. Remove all.
I. Lack of proper ridge.
J. Dermoid sinus, aggression,
hip dysplasia, hypothyroid-
ism, lumbo-sacral transi-
tional vertebrae, cervical
vertebral instability,
achalasia.

131. ROTTWEILER
A. Disinterested or aggressive,
often must muzzle.
B. Low sex drive.
C. Seven.
D. Twelve to eighteen.
E. May be a bit late, some-
times slow but free whelp-
ers. In some strains lack of

maternal instincts a problem.
F. Remove all.
G. Docked, short, not flush with body but shorter than Dobe, leave one joint.
J. Ectropion, hip dysplasia, atresia ani, entropion, cleft palate, deafness, diabetes mellitus—juvenile onset, von Willebrand's disease, retinal dysplasia.

132. SAINT BERNARD
A. Normal, but cannot support weight of male—need help.
B. Body weight, without muscling or too fat means many AI's. Assisted breedings.
C. Eight to ten.
D. Sixteen.
E. Free whelpers.
F. Remove rears.
J. Ectropion, distichiasis, eversion of nictitating membrane, vaginal hyperplasia and prolapse, lip fold pyoderma, diabetes mellitus, entropion, osteochondritis dessicans, large percentage hip dysplasia, genu valgum, osteogenic sarcoma, gastric torsion, Stockard's paralysis, factor VIII deficiency, factor IX deficiency, epilepsy, ununited anchoneal process, atlanto-axial subluxation, aphakia, corneal dermoid cyst, fibrinogen deficiency, ectasia.

133. SALUKI
A. Puberty two years or more, irregular ovulation. Stress can make them go out.
B. Hold bitches. Loss of libido usually due to hypothyroidism.

C. Five to eight.
D. Sixteen.
E. Free whelpers, but like their people around.
F. All usually removed.
J. Umbilical hernias, bad bites, cryptorchidism, corneal dermoid cyst, stress-triggered ailments, barbiturate hypersensitivity, hypothyroidism, Marfan syndrome.

134. SAMOYED
A. Puberty one year or more, then normal and regular.
B. Outside ties frequent.
C. Six to seven.
D. Twelve.
E. Slow, but free whelpers, good mothers.
F. Remove rear, if present.
H. Shave and/or tape ears if not standing by twelve weeks.
I. Blue eyes, lack of pigment (eye rims and nose).
J. Cryptorchidism, chondrodysplasia, cleft palate, hip dysplasia, retinal atrophy—general progressive, factor VIII deficiency, pulmonic valve stenosis, intervertebral disc disease, atrial septal defect, diabetes mellitus—adult onset, spina bifida, kerratitis sicca, retinal dysplasia.

135. SCHIPPERKE
A. Puberty twelve months or even two years. Some silent seasons.
B. Normal.
C. Four (one to eight).
D. Four to five.
E. Usually free whelpers.
F. Remove all.
G. Docked, flush with rump.

135. SCHIPPERKE (*cont.*)
   J. Bad bites, schistosoma re-
      flexus, entropion, narrow
      palpebral fissure, aseptic
      necrosis of femoral head.

136. SCOTTISH DEERHOUND
   A. Puberty late, otherwise nor-
      mal, eight-to-ten month
      cycle.
   B. Normal and eager.
   C. Eight to nine.
   D. Twelve to twenty-four.
   E. Some primary inertias, but
      generally free whelpers,
      good mothers.
   F. Usually removed.
   I. "Ring" tails, "woollies".
   J. Cryptorchidism, gastric tor-
      sion, pituitary dwarfism, os-
      teochondritis dessicans,
      pancreatitis, immune
      disorders.

137. SCOTTISH TERRIER
   A. Generally normal, some
      irregularities.
   B. Normal, some AI's or ele-
      vations needed for short
      legs.
   C. Four to five.
   D. Seven to nine.
   E. Large pup heads and some
      primary inertia—some
      sections.
   F. Removal optional.
   G. *Not* docked.
   J. Craniomandibular osteopa-
      thy, recurrent tetany, cysti-
      nuria, atopic dermatitis, hy-
      pothyroidism, von Wille-
      brand's disease, histiocy-
      toma, melanoma,
      achondroplasia, deafness,
      lens luxation, pyometra,
      ataxia, thrombopathia, Fac-
      tor IX deficiency.

138. SEALYHAM TERRIER
   A. Longer cycles.
   B. Frequent AI's due to heavy
      bodies and short legs.
   C. Four to five.
   D. Six to eight.
   E. Some easy, stand and go to
      work. Others lazy and need
      assistance. Usually good
      mothers, independent and
      sensible.
   F. Removal optional.
   G. Docked, leave one half.
   I. Ears too small.
   J. Lacrimal duct atresia,
      atopy, retinal dysplasia,
      lens luxation, deafness, te-
      tralogy of Fallot,
      microphthalmia.

139. SAR PLANINETZ
A.–D. Similar to the Castro
      Laboreiro.

140. SHAR PEI
   A. May only be fertile in fall
      heat; silent heats, many
      AI's.
   B. Low libido, possibly due to
      low thyroid, sometimes a
      problem. Many AI's in
      some lines, others normal.
   C. Five.
   D. Fourteen to sixteen.
   E. Free whelpers, often fifty-
      eight to fifty-nine days.
      Good mothers, wean pups
      early.
   F. Rear removed, if present.
   I. Too long coats, tongue not
      black, "flowered" spotting.
   J. Bad bites, umbilical her-
      nias, hypothyroidism
      (ninety percent of breed),
      severe entropion, hip dys-
      plasia, overbite, patellar
      luxation, inguinal hernia.

141. SHETLAND SHEEPDOG
   A. Variable estrus and ovulation. Immature tract; not willing, especially when sent away.
   B. Normal.
   C. Four to six.
   D. Six to ten.
   E. Free whelpers, good mothers.
   F. Remove all.
   H. Tape or glue, if not tipped by eight weeks.
   I. Oversized, mismarks, wall eye.
   J. Cryptorchidism, trichiasis, retinal atrophy—central progressive, microphthalmia, choroidal hypoplasia, cataract, factor VIII deficiency, estasia, hip dysplasia, nasal solar dermatitis, achondroplasia, patent ductus arteriosus, patellar luxation, aseptic necrosis of the femoral head, deafness, tarsal subluxation, hypothyroidism, epilepsy, von Willebrand's disease, Factor IX deficiency.

142. SHIBA INU
   A. Normal.
   B. Normal, eager breeders.
   C. Four.
   D. Eight to ten.
   E. One scream at birth, free whelpers. Good mothers.
   J. Short spine, bad bites.

143. SHIH TZU
   A. Irregular cycles, won't stand first time.
   B. Sometimes "rough up" bitches. Sometimes shorter.
   C. Three to six.
   D. Four to six.

   E. Free whelpers, but long—six hours till live pup.
   F. Remove all.
   I. Unpigmented nose and eye rims, blue eyes.
   J. Renal cortical hypoplasia, clefts of lip and palate, intervertebral disc disease, entropion.

144. SIBERIAN HUSKY
   A. Often difficult, muzzle and assistant necessary.
   B. Normal, eager.
   C. Three to seven.
   D. Twelve to sixteen.
   E. Free whelpers, but slow. Don't panic—ten to twelve hours for six pups common. May have diarrhea and deteriorate in condition during lactation.
   F. Remove all.
   J. Cryptorchidism, hip dysplasia, factor VIII deficiency, retinal atrophy—general progressive, corneal dystrophy, cataracts, ventricular septal defects.

145. SILKY TERRIER
   A. Silent heats common, also false pregnancies.
   B. Normal.
   C. Two to five.
   D. One to two.
   E. Sections sometimes necessary. Eclampsia may be problem during pregnancy.
   F. Remove all.
   G. Docked, leave one-third of tail (about half an inch at four days—end of tan mark).
   I. White coats.
   J. Cryptorchidism, cleft palates, atresia ani, gycogen

145. SILKY TERRIER (*cont.*)
    storage disease, collapsed
    trachea, atlanto-axial sub-
    luxation, hydrocephalus,
    occipital dysplasia, patellar
    luxation, aseptic necrosis of
    femoral head, diabetes,
    congenital cardiovascular
    defects, epilepsy.

146. SKYE TERRIER
    A. Normal.
    B. Normal.
    C. Six.
    D. Eight to ten.
    E. Free whelpers, although a
       bit slow. Good mothers.
    I. Kinked tail end.
    J. Missing teeth, bad bites,
       urine leakers, "juvenile
       limp," foramen magnum
       enlargement, ulcerative co-
       litis, laryngeal hypoplasia
       and collapse,
       hypothyroidism.

147. SOFT-COATED WHEATEN
    TERRIER
    A. Normal.
    B. Normal.
    C. Five to seven.
    D. Seven to eleven.
    E. Free whelpers, but make
       sure they're done.
    F. Remove all.
    G. Docked, leave two-thirds
       (short back, thick tail) or
       one half (long back, thin tail).
    I. Light eyes, lack of proper
       Wheaten color.
    J. Bad bites, missing teeth,
       cataract, retinal atrophy—
       progressive, hip dysplasia,
       von Willebrand's disease.

148. SPINONI ITALIANI
    A. Normal.
    B. Normal.

C. Eight to ten.
D. Sixteen.
E. Free whelpers.
G. Dock, leave just under half
   of tail.

149. STAFFORDSHIRE BULL
    TERRIER
    A. Normal.
    B. Normal.
    C. Seven.
    D. Eight.
    E. Free whelpers, good
       mothers.
    J. Bad bites, cataracts—juve-
       nile, entropion, clefts of lip
       and palate.

150. STANDARD POODLE
    A. Late puberty fourteen to
       eighteen months, normal.
    B. Normal and eager early.
    C. Six to twelve.
    D. Sixteen.
    E. Free whelpers, good
       mothers.
    F. Remove all.
    G. Docked, leave about half of
       tail, or just short of top of
       head.
    J. Bad bites, umbilical her-
       nias, distichiasis, epiphora,
       hip dysplasia, iris atrophy,
       microphthalmia, cataract—
       juvenile, entropion, retinal
       atrophy—progressive, epi-
       lepsy, patent ductus arterio-
       sus, osteogenesis imper-
       fecta, gastric torsion,
       deafness, intervertebral
       disc disease, von Wille-
       brand's disease.

151. STANDARD SCHNAUZER
    A. Normal.
    B. Normal.
    C. Six to eight.
    D. Seven to twelve.

E. Normal.

F. Removal all.

G. Docked, just at end of tan (light) mark.

H. Cropped at six to ten weeks, slightly longer than miniature; graceful, no bell.

I. Late eruption of baby teeth, forty to fifty days.

J. Underbites, hip dysplasia, Schnauzer comodome syndrome, pulmonic stenosis, perianal adenoma.

152. SUSSEX SPANIEL

A. Skipped seasons or one estrus per year; variable ovulation time.

B. Frequent absence of interest—kennel with bitch or testosterone injection two to four days prior to breeding date.

C. Two to eight.

D. Four to six.

E. Never leave alone—don't open sacs, etc. After delivery, good mothers. Often lose up to half litter in first two weeks due to genetic and respiratory problems. Eyes open three weeks, slow development.

F. Remove all.

G. Docked, leave generous one-third (or about two-fifths).

J. Underbites, intervertebral disc disease, many breeding problems, heart murmurs and enlarged hearts.

153. TIBETAN MASTIFF

A. Normal, cycle once a year in fall.

B. Normal.

C. Seven to eight (more males than females).

D. Under twelve—grow rapidly!

E. Free whelpers, very rough and protective. Owners may not see pups for two weeks. Mother weans and culls herself.

F. Remove rear only.

J. Peripheral nerve disease.

154. TIBETAN SPANIEL

A. Normal, once per year.

B. Normal.

C. Three to four.

D. Four to five.

E. Free whelpers, but *need* owners, no kennel.

I. Underbites normal.

J. Umbilical hernias.

155. TIBETAN TERRIER

A. Normal.

B. Normal.

C. Five to six (more males).

D. Four to five.

E. Normal, free whelpers, good mothers.

F. Removal optional.

I. Slow to cut teeth.

J. Underbites penalized, von Willebrand's disease.

156. TOY POODLE

A. Sometimes canal too small and short for adequate tie.

B. Good, may have to be held or elevated on book, etc. if height difference.

C. Two to three.

D. Three to six.

E. Generally free whelpers, unless very tiny or single-pup litter. Some lines slow and need help. Good mothers, unless too nervous.

F. Remove all.

G. Docked, leave nearly two-

156. TOY POODLE (*cont.*)
thirds; do at five or even
seven days if very tiny.
  I. Oversize, gay tails.
  J. Distichiasis, underbites,
  atopic dermatitis, hydrocephalus, ectasia, retinal
  atrophy—general progressive, patent ductus arteriosus, plantaris muscle fibrosis, hyperadrenocorticism,
  retinal dysplasia, kerratitis
  sicca, cataract—juvenile,
  entropion, collapsed trachea, deafness, clefts of lip
  and palate, aseptic necrosis
  of femoral head.

157. VIZSLA
  A. Normal.
  B. Normal, but may be shy
  with owners around.
  C. Six to eight.
  D. Ten to fourteen.
  E. Free whelpers, good mothers, protective.
  F. Remove all.
  G. Docked, leave generous two
  thirds.
  I. Too much white, black
  nose, very light eyes.
  J. Cryptorchidism, bad bites,
  ectropion, factor VIII deficiency, hip dysplasia, osteosarcoma, chronic pancreatitis, epilepsy,
  entropion, retinal atrophy—general progressive,
  craniomandibular osteopathy, facial nerve paralysis,
  cataract—juvenile, shy
  temperaments, von Willebrand's disease,
  hypofibrinogenemia.

158. WEIMARANER
  A. Normal.

  B. Eager breeders, males don't
  tolerate one another.
  C. Six to nine.
  D. Ten to sixteen.
  E. Free whelpers, good mothers. Pups often born with
  dark stripes that disappear.
  F. Remove all.
  G. Docked, leave about half
  tail (one and one-half
  inches), at taper or to cover
  genitals.
  I. Long coats, pink eye and
  nose pigment, white
  markings.
  J. Underbites, cryptorchidism,
  umbilical hernias, eversion
  of nictitating membrane,
  hip dysplasia, gastric torsion, entropion, factor VIII
  deficiency, syringomyelia,
  ununited anchoneal pro-
  cess, corneal dermoid cyst,
  hypertrophic osteodystrophy, missing brains, distichiasis, Factor XI
  deficiency.

159. WELSH SPRINGER
SPANIEL
  A. Normal.
  B. Normal.
  C. Four to six.
  D. Eight to twelve.
  E. Free whelpers, good
  mothers.
  F. Remove all.
  G. Docked, leave one third.
  J. Underbites, epilepsy, azo-
  spermia, hip dysplasia.

160. WELSH TERRIER
  A. Normal.
  B. Normal.
  C. Five to six.
  D. Four to nine.

E. Normal, good mothers.

F. Remove all.

G. Docked, to level of top of head—leave three quarters. Fat tail bit longer, thin tail bit shorter.

J. Distichiasis, lens luxation, patellar luxation.

161. WEST HIGHLAND WHITE TERRIER

A. Normal.

B. Lazy, not always eager.

C. Three to four.

D. Six.

E. Slow, lazy whelpers, some cesareans due to small pelvis or because birth is too slow. A few indifferent mothers.

F. Remove all.

G. Do not dock!!

H. Clip ear hair at three months or tape at five months if ears not erect.

I. Mismarks, lack of nose pigment.

J. Retained baby teeth, cryptorchidism, bad bites, aseptic necrosis of femoral head, craniomandibular osteopathy, globoid cell leukodystrophy, atopic dermatitis, inguinal hernia, myothonia, hypothyroidism, hydrocephalus.

162. WHIPPET

A. Normal, late puberty.

B. Normal.

C. Four to eight.

D. Eight to twelve.

E. Very few problems.

F. Remove all.

I. Light eyes.

J. Cryptorchidism, overbites, color mutant alopecia, stool eating, coliform enteritis, ectodermal defect, sebaceous adenoma, hypersensitivity to barbiturates and insecticides.

163. WIRE-HAIRED POINTING GRIFFON

A. Normal. May scream when bred.

B. Normal.

C. Six to eight.

D. Sixteen.

E. Bitches nervous, hard deliveries. Leave them be as much as possible, frequent eclampsia. Pups need lots of socialization.

F. Remove all.

G. Docked, leave generous one-third or more.

I. Oversized, too much chest coat, "Woollies," smooth coats.

J. Hip dysplasia, shy, fear biters.

164. YORKSHIRE TERRIER

A. Normal.

B. Normal, eager.

C. One to four.

D. Four to six.

E. Like owners to help, inertia and eclampsia frequent, twenty percent require cesareans.

F. Remove all.

G. Docked, leave half an inch or just beyond tan mark.

H. Clip hair if not erect by twelve weeks.

I. Failure of black to turn steel gray by one year.

J. Distichiasis, coliform enteritis, anasarca, inguinal her-

164. YORKSHIRE TERRIER
(*cont.*)
nia, schistosoma reflexus,
hypoglycemia—juvenile,
patellar luxation, atlanto-
axial subluxation, kerratitis sicca, aseptic necrosis of
femoral head, hydrocepha-
lus, retinal atrophy—pro-
gressive, collapsed trachea,
enchondromatosis, retinal
dysplasia.

Glossary

GLOSSARY

Key:

SCIENTIFIC NAME
A.   System
B.   Other Names
C.   Inheritance
D.   Description
E.   Comments

   ? = unknown

Note: Categories elminated are not applicable to the particular term.

ACHALASIA
A.   Digestive.
B.   Megaesophagus, dilated esophagus.
C.   Recessive (uncertain).
D.   Esophagus dilated all the way to stomach: vomiting begins at weaning.

ACHLORHYDRIA
A.   Digestive.
C.   ?
D.   Lack of hydrocholoric acid in stomach for digestion.

ACHONDROPLASIA
A.   Bone.
B.   Dwarfism.
C.   Recessive.
D.   Abnormally shortened long bones.

ANASARCA
A.   Blood/vascular.
B.   "Walrus puppy," "rubber puppy," "water puppy."
C.   ?
D.   Lethal generalized edema of newborn: huge size usually requires cesarean delivery.

ANURY (BRACHURY)
A.   Bone.
C.   Recessive.
D.   Lack of any tail (or a very short tail).

APHAKIA
A.   Eye.
C.   Recessive.
D.   Absence of lens, often associated with other eye abnormalities.

ASEPTIC NECROSIS OF THE FEMORAL HEAD
A.   Bone.
B.   Legg-Calve-Perthes disease.
C.   ?
D.   Reduced blood supply to hip joint, degeneration and re-modeling, limping and pain.
E.   More common in smaller breeds.

ATAXIA
A.   CNS.
C.   Recessive.
D.   Born normal, lose control of limbs by four to six months.

ATLANTO-AXIAL SUBLUXATION
A.   Bone.
B.   Hypoplasia of dens.
C.   ?
D.   Malformed first two neck vertebra slip and press on cord: neck pain to total quadriplegia.
E.   Occurs mostly in toy breeds.

ATOPIC DERMATITIS
A. Skin.
B. Contact allergy.
C. ?
D. Itching and self-mutilation: may be an immunological disorder.

ATRIAL SEPTAL DEFECT
A. Blood/vascular.
C. Polygenic.
D. Hole between two upper heart chambers: murmur, severe lack of oxygen, weakness.

AZOSPERMIA
A. Genital.
C. ?
D. Spermatogenic arrest: sudden sterility.

BITHORACIC ECTOMELIA
A. Bone.
C. Recessive.
D. Lack of front legs.
E. Very rare.

BLACK HAIR FOLLICULAR DYSPLASIA
A. Skin.
C. ?
D. Black areas on body have abnormal hair, white areas normal.

CALCINOSIS CIRCUMSCRIPTA
A. Skin.
B. Calcium gout.
C. ?
D. Lumps in skin caused by calcium deposits.

CARPAL SUBLUXATION
A. Bone.
C. Recessive, sex-linked.
D. Wrists out of joint.
E. This gene is allelic to one for hemophilia A.

CATARACT—UNILATERAL
A. Eye.
C. ?
D. Lens opacity occurs in only one eye.

CATARACT WITH MICROPHTHALMIA
A. Eye.
C. ?
D. Cataract associated with abnormally small eyes, often present at birth.

CATARACTS—BILATERAL
A. Eye.
B. Triangular, subcapsular cataracts.
C. Dominant (incomplete penetrance).
D. Opaque lenses form in both eyes, usually after two years.

CATARACTS—JUVENILE
A. Eye.
C. Recessive.
D. Bilateral lens opacities by age one or two, total blindness.

CEREBELLAR CORTICAL ABIOTROPHY
A. CNS.
B. Neuroonal abiotrophy.
C. Recessive.
D. Starts at eight weeks, weakness leading to total paralysis.

CEREBELLAR HYPOPLASIA
A. CNS.
C. ?
D. Abnormal gait and loss of control starting at about twelve weeks.

CEREBRO-SPINAL DEMYELINIZATION
A. CNS.
C. ?

D. Progressive degeneration of spine.

CERVICAL VERTEBRAL INSTABILITY
A. Bone.
B. "CVI," "wobbler."
C. ?
D. Unstable vertebra in lower neck: weakness, incoordination, may lead to paralysis.

CHONDRODYSPLASIA
A. Bone.
B. Dwarf.
C. Recessive.
D. Shortened, deformed front legs with downhill posture.

CHOROIDAL HYPOPLASIA
A. Eye.
C. ?
D. Mild disease of back of eye, usually symptomless.

CHRONIC PANCREATITIS
A. Digestive.
B. Pancreatic atrophy.
C. ?
D. Lack of enzymes that digest fat and protein, gray greasy stools, chronic weight loss despite appetite.

CLEFTS OF LIP AND PALATE
A. Bone.
C. May not always be genetic.
D. Nonclosure of bones of upper jaw and roof of mouth.

COLIFORM ENTERITIS
A. Digestive.
C. ?
D. Persistent, nervous diarrhea.

COLLAPSED TRACHEA
A. Respiratory.
C. ?
D. Improperly formed windpipe

cartilage collapses: dry "honk" cough, blue on exercise.

COLOR MUTANT ALOPECIA
A. Skin.
B. Blue dog dermatitis.
C. Recessive.
D. Hyperkeretinization and alopecia associated with the D (dilute) color gene.
E. Can be seen in blues (dilute of black) or "fawns" (light gray dilute of red).

COPPER TOXICOSIS
A. Digestive.
B. Chronic progressive hepatitis, Wilson's disease.
C. ?
D. Selective accumulation of copper in the liver leading to liver failure.

CORNEAL DERMOID CYST
A. Eye.
C. ?
D. Congenital cyst on eye surface containing sweat and oil glands plus hair.

CORNEAL DYSTROPHY
A. Eye.
B. Corneal leukoma.
C. ?
D. White scarring of eye surface.

CORNEAL ULCER
A. Eye.
C. ?
D. Superficial erosion of cornea, resistant to treatment. May be more common in spayed females.

CRANIOMANDIBULAR OSTEOPATHY
A. Bone.
B. Lion jaw, hog jaw, "CMO."
C. Recessive (uncertain).

CRANIOMANDIBULAR
OSTEOPATHY (cont.)
D. Thickened lower jaw in pups,
pain, fever, goes away with
age if they don't starve first.

CRANIOSCHISIS
A. Bone.
C. Recessive (lethal).
D. Congenital fissures in skull
bones, brain or its mem-
branes herniate through.

CRYPTORCHIDISM
A. Genital.
B. Undescended testicle(s).
C. ?
D. Bilaterals sterile, unilaterals
fertile but barred from
showing.
E. Widespread in many breeds.

CUTANEOUS ASTHENIA
A. Skin.
B. Ehlers-Danlos syndrome.
C. Dominant (uncertain).
D. Fragile skin that overstretches
and tears easily.

CYCLIC NEUTROPENIA
A. Blood/vascular.
B. Gray Collie syndrome.
C. Recessive.
D. Lethal, associated with silver/
white color gene, cycles of
very low white-cell counts
lead to overwhelming
infections.

CYSTINURIA
A. Urinary.
C. Recessive, sex-linked.
D. High cystine excreted in
urine, prone to stone formation; symptoms seen only in
males.

DEAFNESS
A. Ear.

C. Dominant (homozygous
merles).
D. Born without ability to hear.
E. Doesn't occur in
heterozygote.

DEAFNESS
A. Ear.
C. Recessive.
D. Born without ability to hear,
often associated with white
color, especially white heads
and ears.

DEFORMED THIRD CERVICAL
VERTEBRA
A. Bone.
C. ?
D. Spinal cord pressure in neck,
incoordination starting at
three to six months.

DEGENERATIVE MYELOPATHY
A. Muscle.
B. Necrotizing myelopathy.
C. ?
D. Muscle wasting of aged dogs,
progressive ataxia.

DEMODECTIC MANGE—
GENERALIZED
A. Skin.
B. Red mange, puppy mange.
C. ?
D. T-cell deficiency (uncertain),
some highly resistant to
treatment.

DERMOID SINUS
A. Skin.
C. ?
D. Tubelike cyst on back, usually
communicates with spinal
cord.
E. Associated with hair "ridge."

DIABETES MELLITUS—
JUVENILE ONSET
A. Endocrine.

B. Sugar diabetes.
C. ?
D. Low insulin production; pre-
disposition in some breeds.

DIABETES MELLITUS—
JUVENILE ONSET
A. Endocrine.
B. Sugar diabetes.
C. Recessive.
D. Onset of insulin deficiency at
two to six months.

DISTICHIASIS
A. Eye.
B. "Double eyelashes."
C. ?
D. Extra row of lashes, usually
on lower lid, irritate eye
surface.

ECTASIA SYNDROME
A. Eye.
B. "Collie eye," optic nerve
hypoplasia.
C. Recessive.
D. Multiple abnormalities of
optic disc and retina.
E. Occurs in several breeds.

ECTODERMAL DEFECT
A. Skin.
C. ?
D. Symmetrical areas of hairless-
ness, up to two-thirds of
body.

ECTROPION
A. Eye.
B. Loose lids.
C. ?
D. Hanging lower lids create red,
inflamed eyes.
E. Common in many breeds.

ELBOW JOINT DEFORMITY
A. Bone.
C. ?
D. Deformed joint surface in the
elbow.

ELONGATED SOFT PALATE/
STENOTIC NARES
A. Respiratory.
C. ?
D. Pinched nostrils and ob-
structed airway: snoring, gag-
ging, lack of exercise
tolerance.
E. Common in brachycephalic
breeds.

ENCHONDROMATOSIS
A. Bone.
C. ?
D. Multiple cartilage exostoses
(bumps) on bones near joints
and on ribs, may cause incoordination if severe.

ENOSTOSIS
A. Bone.
B. Juvenile osteomyelitis, eosin-
ophilic panostitis, "Pano."
C. ?
D. Acute shifting lameness of
growing dogs, deep bone
pain, self-limiting.

ENTROPION
A. Eye.
B. "Diamond eye."
C. ?
D. Eyelids roll in, causing hair to
rub on eye, can lead to
blindness.
E. Occurs in many breeds.

EOSINOPHILIC COLITIS
A. Digestive.
B. Ulcerative colitis.
C. ?
D. Chronic bouts of diarrhea.

EPILEPSY
A. CNS.
C. Recessive, in some breeds.
D. Recurrent seizures, with onset
at one to three years.

EPILEPSY (*cont.*)
E. Some epilepsy is not hereditary.

EPIPHYSEAL DYSPLASIA
A. Bone.
B. Recessive.
C. ?
D. Bone growth disorder causing swaying, sagging rear legs.

FACTOR II DEFICIENCY
A. Blood/vascular.
B. Hypoprothrombinemia.
C. ?
D. Clotting, disorder, severe nosebleeds.

FACTOR VII DEFICIENCY
A. Blood/vascular.
C. Recessive (uncertain).
D. Lack of blood-clotting factor number VII, usually symptomless.
E. Also reported to be an incomplete dominant.

FACTOR VIII DEFICIENCY
A. Blood/vascular.
B. Hemophilia A, AHF deficiency.
C. Recessive, sex-linked.
D. Slowed clotting time, hemorrhagic episodes.

FACTOR IX DEFICIENCY
A. Blood/vascular.
B. Hemophilia B, PTT deficiency, "Christmas disease."
C. Recessive, sex-linked.
D. Prolonged clotting time; heterozygotes bleed more than in hemophilia A.

FACTOR X DEFICIENCY
A. Blood/vascular.
C. Dominant, incomplete penetrance.
D. Severe bleeding in newborns and young adults.
E. More severe in homozygote.

FACTOR XI DEFICIENCY
A. Blood/vascular.
C. Probably incomplete dominant.
D. Minor bleeding episodes.

FANCONI SYNDROME
A. Urinary.
C. Recessive (uncertain).
D. Kidney tubule degeneration, losing first sugar then protein and salts; leads to kidney failure.

FIBRINOGEN DEFICIENCY
A. Blood/vascular.
B. Hypofibrinogenemia.
C. Dominant, incomplete.
D. A minor bleeding disorder.

FLY-BITING SYNDROME
A. CNS.
C. ?
D. Dogs jump up and bite at imaginary flies.

FORAMEN MAGNUM ENLARGEMENT
A. Bone.
C. ?
D. Malformed occipital bone causes pressure on brain, may cause incoordination.

FREIDREICH'S ATAXIA
A. CNS.
C. ?
D. Sclerosis of lower spinal cord, ataxia.

GANGLIOSIDOSIS
A. CNS.
B. Amaurotic idiocy.
C. Recessive.
D. Born normal, become dull and blind at one year with staggering, then seizures.

GASTRIC TORSION
A. Digestive.

B. Bloat/torsion, twisted stomach.
C. ?
D. Stomach rotates on its long axis, shutting off intake and exit; can quickly lead to shock and death.
E. More common in deep-chested, narrow-chested, or extreme "tuck-up" breeds.

GENERALIZED MYOPATHY
A. Muscle.
C. Recessive, sex-linked.
D. Starts at eight weeks; stiff gait, muscle atrophy, swollen tongue, inability to swallow.

GINGIVAL HYPERPLASIA
A. Digestive.
D. Thickening and overgrowth of gums.

GLAUCOMA—PRIMARY
A. Eye.
C. Recessive.
D. Increased fluid pressure in eye leads to pain and blindness.

GLOBOID CELL LEUKODYSTROPHY
A. CNS.
B. Krabbe's disease.
C. Recessive.
D. Progressive stiffness and ataxia.

GLOSSOPHARYNGEAL DEFECT
A. Digestive.
B. "Bird tongue."
C. Recessive (lethal).
D. Abnormally shaped tongue and inability to swallow.

GOITER
A. Endocrine.
C. Dominant.
D. Enlarged thyroid gland.

HAIRLESSNESS
A. Skin.
C. Dominant.
D. Occurs only in heterozygote; homozygous state lethal with severe abnormalities of mouth and throat.
E. This is the gene that produces the Mexican Hairless and Chinese Crested breeds.

HEMERALOPIA
A. Eye.
B. Day blindness.
C. Recessive.
D. Reduced ability to see in bright light.

HEMIVERTEBRA
A. Bone.
B. Butterfly vertebra.
C. ?
D. Some vertebra are short and compressed; from no symptoms to pain, incoordination, and curvature.
E. Most common in "screw-tail" breeds.

HINDQUARTER TREMBLING
A. CNS.
C. ?
D. Permanent but not progressive.

HIP DYSPLASIA
A. Bone.
C. Polygenic.
D. Progressive, developmental deformity of hip joints; symptomless to crippling.

HISTIOCYTOMA
A. Skin.
C. ?
D. Reticulo-endothelial tumor.

HYDROCEPHALUS
A. CNS.
B. "Water on the brain."
C. Several recessives.

HYDROCEPHALUS (*cont.*)
D. Increased fluid pressure within brain damages and destroys nerves.

HYPERADRENOCORTICISM
A. Endocrine.
B. Cushing's syndrome.
C. ?
D. Excess steroid from adrenal gland: potbelly, hair loss, weakness, increased thirst and urination.

HYPERTROPHIC OSTEODYSTROPHY
A. Bone.
B. HOD
C. ?
D. Painful swollen joints and long bones, fever, etc., outgrow disease but may retain some deformity.
E. Most prevalent in giant breeds and associated with oversupplementation.

HYPOGLYCEMIA—JUVENILE
A. Endocrine.
C. ?
D. Sudden low blood sugar due to stress; ataxia and convulsions; treatable, puppy disease.
E. Most common in toys.

HYPOSPADIA
A. Genital.
C. ?
D. Open sheath and abnormally developed penis.

INGUINAL HERNIA
A. Muscle.
B. Rupture.
C. ?
D. Bulging of abdominal contents in groin area.
E. Seen only in female dogs.

INTERTARSAL SUBLUXATION
A. Bone.
C. ?
D. Overangulated hock with subluxation, unstable joint, and lameness.

INTERVERTEBRAL DISC DISEASE
A. Bone.
B. Slipped disc.
C. ?
D. Disc(s) between vertebrae rupture and press on spinal cord: pain, weakness to paralysis of limbs.
E. Can occur in neck or back.

KERRATITIS SICCA
A. Eye.
B. "KCS," "dry eye."
C. ?
D. Lack of or loss of ability to produce tears: leads to severe eye damage.

KIDNEY APLASIA, UNILATERAL
A. Urinary.
C. ?
D. Born with only one functional kidney.
E. May be symptomless.

LACRIMAL DUCT ATRESIA
A. Eye.
B. Tearing.
C. ?
D. Deficiency in ducts that drain away tears, thus drainage of tears down face.

LARYNGEAL HYPOPLASIA
A. Respiratory.
B. Collapsed larynx.
C. Recessive.
D. Voice box improperly developed, collapses, breathing difficulties.

LENS LUXATION
A. Eye.
C. ?
D. Lens slips out of position: leads to secondary glaucoma.

LISSENCEPHALY
A. CNS.
C. ?
D. Born with few if any convolutions in brain: severe retardation.

LYMPHEDEMA
A. Blood/vascular.
C. Dominant.
D. Pitting edema of hind legs in pups, usually outgrow but can be fatal.

MACROCYTIC ANEMIA
A. Blood/vascular.
C. Recessive.
D. Associated with genetic dwarfs; pleiotropic effect of recessive dwarf gene.

MALABSORPTION SYNDROME
A. Digestive.
C. ?
D. Congenital or acquired inability to absorb digested food: leads to starvation.

MARFAN SYNDROME
A. Reticulo-endothelial.
C. ?
D. Hereditary disorder including displaced eye lens and thin, elongated toes ("spider toes").

MASTOCYTOMA
A. Skin.
C. ?
D. Malignant and often rapidly spreading nodular skin tumors.

MELANOMA
A. Skin.
C. ?
D. Malignant tumor of pigment cells, often dark in color, in mouth or on skin.

MICROPHTHALMIA
A. Eye.
C. Dominant (homozygous merles).
D. Born with small, nonfunctional eyes.
E. Doesn't occur in heterozygote.

MITRAL VALVE DEFECT
A. Blood/vascular.
C. ?
D. Defect in valve between upper and lower heart chambers: murmur, weakness.

MONONEPHROSIS
A. Urinary.
C. Recessive (homozygote lethal).
D. Cystic degeneration of one kidney.

NASAL SOLAR DERMATITIS
A. Skin.
B. "Collie nose."
C. ?
D. Lack of pigment plus sunlight allergy causes blistering and erosion on top of nose.
E. Occurs in several breeds.

NEUROMAL CEROID LIPOFUSCINOSIS
A. CNS.
B. Juvenile amaurotic idiocy, "Batten's disease."
C. Recessive.
D. Progressive ataxia and mental dullness starting at two to three months.

NEUORONAL
GLYCOPROTEINOSIS
A. CNS.
B. Lafora's disease.
C. Recessive.
D. Seizures and mental deterioration starting at five months.

NEUROTROPIC OSTEOPATHY
A. CNS.
B. Foot chewing.
C. Recessive.
D. Loss of feeling in feet leads to foot chewing and mutilation.

NICTITATING MEMBRANE EVERSION
A. Eye.
C. Recessive (uncertain).
D. Haw rolls out and its gland is red and prominent.

OLIGODENDROGLIOMA
A. CNS.
C. ?
D. Slow-growing brain tumor (benign).

OLIGODONTIA
A. Bone.
C. Recessive.
D. Congenital lack of many or most teeth.

OPTIC NERVE HYPOPLASIA
A. Eye.
C. ?
D. Lack of development of optic nerve: blindness.

OSTEOCHONDRITIS DESSICANS
A. Bone.
B. Shoulder dysplasia.
C. ?
D. Growth disorder of cartilage: pain, lameness.

OSTEOCHONDROSIS OF SPINE
A. Bone.
B. "Runners."

C. ?
D. Bone/cartilage degeneration in back: arched back, hips higher than shoulders, stilted gait.

OSTEOGENESIS IMPERFECTA
A. Bone.
B. "Snowshoe" feet.
C. ?
D. Abnormal bone development: flat feet, elbows out, knock-knees, loose ligaments.

OSTEOGENIC SARCOMA
A. Bone.
C. ?
D. Malignant bone tumor.
E. More frequent in giant breeds.

OSTEOPETROSIS
A. Bone.
C. ?
D. Puppies mistaken for "swimmers," abnormally dense bone.

OTOCEPHALIC SYNDROME
A. Bone.
C. Recessive.
D. Low-grade—lack of jaw and hydrocephalus; high-grade—no structures in front of brain stem.
E. Very rare.

OVERBITE
A. Bone.
B. Overshot jaw, parrot mouth, shark jaw.
C. ?
D. Upper jaw longer than under jaw, resulting in malocclusion of teeth.

PANNUS
A. Eye.
C. ?
D. Vessels, skin, and pigment

migrate over eye surface, leading to blindness.

E. Usual genetic form starts at outside and moves toward inside; "atypical pannus" starts at inside and grows toward outside.

PATELLAR LUXATION
A. Bone.
B. Slipped knees.
C. ?
D. Knee cap slips out of its groove; symptomless to crippling, can be either outward or inward.

PATENT DUCTUS ARTERIOSUS
A. Blood/vascular.
C. Polygenic threshold.
D. Failure of the fetal aorta-pulmonary artery shunt to close: loud murmur, exercise intolerance.

PERIANAL FISTULA
A. Digestive.
C. ?
D. Open draining tracts around anal orifice.

PERSISTENT PUPILLARY MEMBRANE
A. Eye.
C. Dominant, range of expression.
D. Strands of tissue across pupil: may be symptomless or lead to opacities.

PERSISTENT RIGHT AORTIC ARCH
A. Blood/vascular.
C. Polygenic (uncertain).
D. Abnormal artery constricts esophagus half way to stomach: vomiting.

PITUITARY CYSTS
A. Endocrine.

C. ?
D. Can lead to obesity, genital atrophy, and water diabetes.
E. Most common in brachycephalic breeds.

PITUITARY DWARFISM
A. Endocrine.
B. "Cretins."
C. ?
D. Normally proportioned dwarf, mentally retarded; the condition is usually fatal.

PITUITARY TUMOR
A. CNS.
C. ?
D. Brain tumor.

PLANTARIS MUSCLE FIBROSIS
A. Muscle.
B. "Hoppers."
C. ?
D. Certain leg muscles degenerate; dog can move only by hopping.

POLYOSTOTIC FIBROUS DYSPLASIA
A. Bone.
C. ?
D. Bone cysts form in wrist area.

PRIMARY UTERINE INERTIA
A. Genital.
C. ?
D. At term, cervix dilates but uterine contractions never begin.

PSEUDOHERMAPHRODITE
A. Genital.
C. ?
D. Male form has testes, vulva, and os penis; female form has ovaries, vagina, and penis.
E. Usually sterile.

PULMONIC STENOSIS
A. Blood/vascular.

PULMONIC STENOSIS (*cont.*)
C. Polygenic.
D. Artery from heart to lungs narrow at origin: right heart enlargement, murmur.

PYLORIC STENOSIS
A. Digestive.
C. ?
D. Spasm of stomach exit valve: projectile vomiting.

PYRUVATE KINASE DEFICIENCY
A. Blood/vascular.
B. "PKD," hemolytic anemia.
C. Recessive.
D. Bleeding disorder.

QUADRIPLEGIA WITH AMBLYOPIA
A. CNS.
C. Recessive (lethal).
D. Progressive paralysis with blindness.

RADIUS CURVUS
A. Bone.
B. Bow legs, fiddle front.
C. ?
D. Extreme bowing caused by uneven growth rates of the two lower front leg bones.

RECURRENT TETANY
A. CNS.
B. "Scottie cramp."
C. Recessive.
D. When excited, dog has stiff gait, not progressive.
E. Occurs in several breeds.

RENAL CORTICAL HYPOPLASIA
A. Urinary.
C. ?
D. Degeneration of both kidneys, beginning at about one year.

RETINAL ATROPHY—CENTRAL PROGRESSIVE
A. Eye.
B. Central PRA, CPRA.

C. Dominant, incomplete penetrance.
D. Retina degenerates, leading to near or total blindness at three to five years.

RETINAL ATROPHY— GENERALIZED PROGRESSIVE
A. Eye.
B. General PRA.
C. Recessive.
D. Retina degenerates, causing first night blindness then total blindness.

RETINAL DYSPLASIA
A. Eye.
B. Retinal dystrophy.
C. Recessive.
D. Retinal detachment, leading to blindness.

SEBORRHEA
A. Skin.
B. Hyperkeratinization, greasy skin disease.
C. ?
D. Increased production of upper skin layers and gland secre- tions: greasy, leathery skin, hard to treat.

SHORT SPINE
A. Bone.
B. "Baboon dogs."
C. Recessive.
D. All vetebra are shortened: dog twice as tall as he is long, compresses soft tissue organs.

SHOULDER DISLOCATION
A. Bone.
B. Slipped shoulder.
C. ?

SPINA BIFIDA
A. Bone.
B. Open spine.

C. Dominant (uncertain).
D. Back bones don't cover nerves properly in lower back: urinary and fecal incontinence, gait abnormalities.
E. More common in tailless breeds.

SPONDYLOLISTHESIS
A. Bone.
C. ?
D. Narrowed channel for spinal cord in mid-neck: may cause pain and lack of coordination.

SPONDYLOSIS DEFORMANS
A. Bone.
C. ?
D. Proliferative, bridging spinal arthritis, ankylosis.

SQUAMOUS CELL CARCINOMA
A. Skin.
C. ?
D. Malignant, erosive skin tumor; occurs on unpigmented areas of body.

STOCKARD'S PARALYSIS
A. Bone.
C. Three dominants.
D. Degeneration of lumbar spine, with partial paralysis beginning at twelve weeks.

SUBAORTIC STENOSIS
A. Blood/vascular.
C. Polygenic.
D. Aorta narrowed below its valve: murmur, enlarged left heart.

SUPERNUMERARY INCISORS
A. Bone.
C. ?
D. Seven incisors in upper jaw.

SYRINGOMYELIA
A. CNS.

B. Spinal dysraphism, "hoppers" disease.
C. ?
D. Dog stands in a crouch and hops to move; nonprogressive.

TETRALOGY OF FALLOT
A. Blood/vascular.
C. Polygenic.
D. Severe heart disorder with four different defects present: murmur, sometimes fatal.

THROMBOPATHIA
A. Blood/vascular.
B. Giant platelet disease.
C. Dominant, incomplete expression.
D. Minor bleeding disorder.

TRACHEAL HYPOPLASIA
A. Respiratory.
C. ?
D. Cartilage rings of windpipe too small: severe lack of exercise tolerance, not surgically correctable.

TRICHIASIS
A. Eye.
C. Dominant, incomplete penetrance.
D. Ingrown extra eyelashes, especially on upper lid, irritate cornea.

UMBILICAL HERNIA
A. Muscle.
B. "Outie," rupture.
C. ?
D. Bulging of abdominal contents at umbilicus.
E. Common, usually harmless.

UNDERBITE
A. Bone.
B. Undershot mouth, Bulldog mouth.

UNDERBITE (*cont.*)

C. ?

D. Lower jaw longer than upper jaw, malocclusion.

E. Desired condition in some breeds.

UNUNITED ANCHONEAL PROCESS

A. Bone.

B. Elbow dysplasia.

C. Three dominants (uncertain).

D. Bone closure failure in elbow joint: pain and limp in front leg(s).

URIC ACID EXCRETION

A. Urinary.

C. Recessive.

D. Prone to form urate stones in bladder.

URINE-DRIBBLING PUPPIES

A. Urinary.

B. "Leakers," "tiddlers."

C. ?

D. Defect in sphincter control at birth.

VENTRICULAR SEPTAL DEFECT

A. Blood/vascular.

C. Polygenic.

D. Hole between two lower heart chambers: pumping deficiency, weak, blue.

VON WILLEBRAND'S DISEASE

A. Blood/vascular.

B. Pseudo-hemophilia.

C. Dominant, variable expression.

D. Bleeding disorder with several abnormal factors.

INDEX

All breeds are listed alphabetically in the Appendix, Breed Specifics and Predispositions, which begins on page 147.

Pages shown in **boldface** contain detailed coverage of the item.